Democratic Discipline in Learning Communities

Theory and Practice

Clifford H. Edwards

ROWMAN & LITTLEFIELD EDUCATION
A division of
ROWMAN & LITTLEFIELD PUBLISHERS, INC.
Lanham • New York • Toronto • Plymouth, UK

Published by Rowman & Littlefield Education
A division of Rowman & Littlefield Publishers, Inc.
A wholly owned subsidary of The Rowman & Littlefield Publishing Group,
Inc.
4501 Forbes Boulevard, Suite 200, Lanham, Maryland 20706
http://www.rowmaneducation.com

Estover Road, Plymouth PL6 7PY, United Kingdom

British Library Cataloguing in Publication Information Available

Library of Congress Cataloging-in-Publication Data
Edwards, Clifford H.
  Democratic discipline in learning communities : theory and practice /
Clifford H. Edwards.
    p. cm.
  Includes bibliographical references.
  ISBN 978-1-60709-984-0 (cloth : alk. paper) -- ISBN 978-1-60709-985-7
(pbk. : alk. paper) -- ISBN 978-1-60709-986-4 (electronic)
  1. School discipline--United States. 2. School improvement programs--
United States. 3. Democracy and education--United States.. I. Title.
  LB3012.2.E39 2010
  371.5--dc22
                                                    2010037978

Printed in the United States of America

Contents

Preface

Discipline problems, including bullying and violence, have for many years been recognized as some of the most significant difficulties schools face. This has been demonstrated in terms of teacher feedback as well as input from society generally. It is the most commonly cited reason given by teachers for leaving the teaching profession. Discipline is not only a very typical problem, it is also identified as the most perverse issue to overcome in teaching.

It is interesting to note that, just as with curriculum proposals, there have been numerous discipline theories and models created over the years. But, despite its critical significance, discipline has rarely been studied with the purpose of finding the best theory. Also, with the exception of behavior modification, research regarding any particular theory or model has not been extensive. No conclusive superiority has been shown for any particular model. Comparative studies are even more scarce.

From an empirical standpoint there is no one theory that stands out as being the best. This is because the criteria used to measure effectiveness are usually expressions of the distinctive characteristics of the approach being studied and cannot be generalized. Thus, data that support one approach may be antithetical to the purposes of another. For example, research on Operant Conditioning may show that administering rewards can cause students to sit quietly while doing their seat work, but fail to promote the development of personal responsibility that is sought in Glasser's Choice Theory. Thus, determining the degree of effectiveness is not simply an empirical matter. There are also philosophical considerations.

Various discipline approaches serve different purposes at a fundamental level, and thus their comparative effectiveness cannot be simply measured using the same set of criteria. Consequently, the effectiveness of any approach has to be determined through carefully designed studies that employ a valid set of criteria unique to that particular model. This means that empirically comparing discipline theories that support different purposes is a fallacious endeavor, and conclusions drawn from such studies are improper.

How then can one determine what theory of discipline to implement? This task is a philosophical one. Teachers must determine the components of their educational philosophy in advance of deciding on methods of discipline. Once educational philosophy has been carefully delineated, teachers can examine various discipline models to determine which most closely fits their philosophy, or perhaps they might be put in a position of having to develop their own set of discipline procedures.

It is often the case that a discipline theory is implemented without first examining the school philosophy or various teachers' individual educational philosophies. This, of course, can cause considerable confusion to teachers and students alike. For one thing, the discipline procedures may be out of harmony with the instructional program. In the confusion, students may experience different expectations from different teachers and run into trouble when they respond incongruously from one class to another or within any particular classroom.

Alarmingly, the fact that teachers in the same school may have significantly different educational philosophies, which likewise may be different from the school philosophy, rarely gets examined for important implications. For example, one teacher may support students' self-direction while another prefers a punishment model. The school, on the other hand, may support teacher control through a system of rewards. Unfortunately, such conditions are common but usually ignored.

The educational philosophy that governs discipline must of necessity be the same as that prescribed for the curriculum. Otherwise there is not only confusion but also general ineffectiveness. Despite the logical necessity of the educational philosophy mapping onto both classroom discipline and the curriculum, they are commonly out of sync. For example, school philosophies often state that students are to be involved in democratic activities while developing self-regulation abilities. However, in these schools, rewards and punishment may be routinely employed, which restrict the development of responsible self-regulation.

In many schools philosophical goals and discipline procedures are completely at odds with each other. Often teachers are unaware of the school philosophy and consequently may engage in discipline practices that are inconsistent with it. The same is typically true of the curriculum and instruction employed. In addition, teachers' own personal educational philosophies are not often articulated, let alone consistently followed. Consequently there may be an absence of declared principles with which to make comparative analyses and guide educational practice.

Some discipline theories do include instructional suggestions. Others fail to mention curricula or the instructional program. In some cases there are blatant philosophical differences between the stated instructional intentions and the discipline procedures. In addition, there are some discipline models that have been criticized because they fail in a fundamental way to employ their stated intentions with regard to discipline. This has been particularly true of most of the so-called democratic discipline models, Glasser's Choice Theory, the Jones Model, and Canter's Assertive Discipline.

The value of having the curriculum and discipline practices consistent with each other seems self-evident, but there is an even more compelling orientation that should be sought—that of making the discipline program an integral part of the curriculum. Consistency and integration are two substantially different characteristics. Consistency refers to the fact that discipline processes and the curriculum are based upon the same set of philosophical principles. For example, appropriate classroom behavior may be promoted through contingencies of reinforcement. These same rewards may be given in the program of instruction. However, discipline and the curriculum may not strictly depend on each other in the way each is implemented.

When the curriculum and discipline are an integral part of each other, they clearly have complete interdependency. There is a perfect matching of intent and operations. One is implemented in the process of employing the other. They depend on each other to be whole and complete. This, of course, is consistency with philosophical principles at the highest level, but also, beyond this, it is a relationship that is full and complete only when curriculum and discipline manifest together in specified ways.

Democratic Discipline in Learning Communities, the model presented in this text, is an example of curriculum and discipline having an integral connection. The reader should keep this in mind while becoming familiar with the learning communities curriculum and how it is integrated with the discipline program.

In reality, discipline is inextricably related to instruction in learning communities. In other words, discipline is effectively implemented within the context of community-based learning experiences. This means, of course, that most of the potential discipline problems can be prevented when integrated instructional processes are employed. Any discipline problems that need to be corrected can be handled within an instructional context where teachers apply the same set of educational principles to both discipline and instruction.

The causes of many discipline problems go unrecognized by teachers, particularly those that they attribute to home and society, but that are in reality a function of the classroom and school generally. Many of these are subtle influences that teachers promote as necessities when in fact they contribute immeasurably to student disruptiveness. For example, many teachers think that student misbehavior must be controlled through rule enforcement, not realizing that these coercive efforts may be the cause of the problem in the first place.

When these constraints promote more disruptiveness, teachers may naively advocate even greater restraint be imposed, thus trying to solve the problem with its cause. It is a common practice, but one that is typically misunderstood. Teachers are more likely to blame parents and society generally rather than assume they are partly at fault themselves for the misbehavior that their controlling actions help create and perpetuate. There are, of course, discipline problems that originate in the school outside their classrooms, or in the home or society generally, with which teachers find difficulty coping. These must be recognized and dealt with appropriately. However, teachers must also recognize that many problems that can and should be prevented originate in their own classrooms.

Ironically, some educators believe that the discipline problems they confront are caused by procedures advocated by others to solve the very same problems. For example, behaviorists presume that one of the primary difficulties suffered by students in school, in terms of school achievement as well as proper discipline, is failure to have controlled reinforcement contingencies in place to routinely regulate their behavior. In contrast, humanistically oriented educators often point out that the controlling strategies embedded in behavioristic techniques are actually the origin of student unruliness.

As already mentioned, humanistic educators believe excessive control is behind much student misbehavior and their failure to achieve up to their potential. The complexity of human systems, particularly the dynamics of complex school environments, makes it extremely difficult to get a clear picture of what is actually happening in a typical classroom. This complexity is not only a function of the differences between students, which are based on their environmentally related inclinations and idiosyncracies, but also the attitudes and values of teachers and administrators and the school environment generally, as well as the home and social culture in which students live. Perhaps because of this complexity, school innovations and modifications have historically involved a limited number of schooling procedures and ignored various other inherently critical factors.

While there have been minor modifications in school curriculum and instruction over the years, there has also been a transition in recommended discipline practices. Punishing rule breakers has been a long-standing traditional approach. Early on this involved the use of corporal punishment. This eventually gave way to what are considered more humane punishments. Thus, unruly children may be required to do extra lessons, copy out the rule violated numerous times, or spend the classroom period in the hallway. They might also lose various privileges, such as participation in school activities such as sports, music, and debate. In extreme cases students might suffer detention or expulsion.

Eventually some educational theorists concluded that punishment was ineffective and instead supported the use of logical consequences to control student behavior. Thus, if a student broke something, he or she had to pay for it rather than suffering some unrelated punishment like staying after school to clean the chalkboards. If a student insisted on standing up rather than sitting down to do his work, his chair might be permanently taken away. The idea seemed to be a good one and is still commonly practiced, but it was eventually discovered that the outcome of consequences was not a matter of what the teacher intended, but rather how students interpreted the consequences and reacted to them. A student could just as well interpret the intended consequence of being isolated from fellow students as punishment when he or she disturbed classmates' study.

Often these students became more disruptive and alienated from their teachers. A similar unexpected phenomenon has been found to operate when teachers attempt to punish their students. Some children find intended punishment to be reinforcing. Instead of a hoped-for reduction in misbehavior, there is a substantial increase. This is true whether teachers intend to punish or provide logical consequences. Again it is not what the teachers intend, but rather how students respond to these stimuli that determines what is actually happening. These results have served to undermine many of the discipline approaches that intend to make discipline more democratic by employing logical consequences. Ironically, the particular procedures used to supply consequences may be the very characteristic that defines the approach as controlling rather than democratic.

As one might predict, providing students with consequences varies depending on the discipline approached used. In some cases, consequences are imposed, while in others students are allowed to help define them. Unfortunately, even in instances where students are given the opportunity to help determine consequences, they may be forcefully imposed by teachers, leaving students to conclude they are simply being controlled. They fail to respond as anticipated because they interpret negative consequences as punitive no matter who creates them.

In addition, many children simply do not want to experience painful consequences and take a far different view of them than teachers intend simply because they don't wish to suffer any kind of discomfort. When this happens, it is easy for them to excuse themselves and blame teachers or the education system even for their own failings. This is especially so when teachers are the ones who impose consequences.

Recognizing conflicts in curricular and discipline practices is essential in determining what the school program should be. It is necessary to have a clear view of the issues and practices along with their assumptions and underlying philosophies. Educators also must know what has happened historically that has shaped the schools. It is critical to understand the purposes of various curricular and discipline efforts and what the outcomes have been. It is particularly important to recognize conflicts between purposes and practices and to clearly delineate what this means in determining an appropriate approach to education.

Because democratic discipline can best be employed within the context of a properly functioning democratic learning community, it is essential that this learning process be correctly conceptualized and the proper teaching and learning principles be put into operation. Democratic principles in education should be an outgrowth of democratic societies generally, with an emphasis on freedom and associated responsibility, along with the development of a moral citizenry.

The operation of democratic learning communities is far different than the way in which schools are generally run. These differences are fundamental and have enormous implications for the teaching process and the nature of learning. To function appropriately in a democratic environment, students must acquire particular attributes that articulate with democratic living, and in the process demonstrate growth in responsible classroom behavior. Also, the attributes of learners in an authentic learning community are far different than those usually exhibited in traditional classrooms. Rather than strictly following teacher directions, students learn with the help of their teachers how to make responsible decisions that lead to learning excellence.

There are defined stages in the development of authentic learning communities. Groups generally struggle to achieve smoothly operating learning communities that have the attributes needed to help prepare students for life in democratic communities outside the classroom. This ordinarily requires considerable time to achieve. However, the time spent in promoting the development of learning communities is worthwhile not only in terms of personal and social growth but also of learning excellence.

In learning communities, students' need satisfaction is of great concern to teachers. In traditional classrooms, however, children usually fulfill very few of their needs. In fact, this imperative is rarely pursued as essential, while in learning communities deliberate efforts are made to promote need satisfaction because it is accepted as fundamentally necessary for children's well-being and academic progress, along with preventing discipline problems. This is done by properly identifying crucial needs and creating strategies to ensure their fulfillment as an integral part of learning community operations.

One of children's most critical needs is that of personal autonomy. In learning communities children are empowered with sufficient autonomy to responsibly direct their own learning. Motivation depends on having the freedom to act according to ones' own desires. But because most needs can only be satisfied within a social context, students must learn that their personal needs can only be achieved as they help their peers fulfill their needs. Helping students accomplish this is a very important teacher responsibility. However, it is difficult at first because of students' inclinations to satisfy their own needs exclusively. They initially seem oblivious to the fact that their needs can't be sufficiently met with a focus only on themselves.

The learning theory that most accurately approximates natural learning is constructivism, which is the theory applied in learning communities. Students are helped to formulate learning plans, along with their peers, that are both interesting to them and fundamentally important in terms of the school curriculum. Though students are given a great deal of decision-making responsibility, teachers must coach them as they gradually learn to make valid, useful decisions about their learning activities. Teachers help their students to engage in sophisticated inquiry learning where they apply appropriate procedures for identifying both social and personal problems to investigate, and learn how to do so with rigor. They are helped not only to identify appropriate learning tasks, but also the means to thoughtfully engage in their research and to draw conclusions from their studies that are supportable given the data they have acquired. This kind of learning orientation is the lifeblood of learning communities and of society generally.

The relationships between students and between students and their teachers are also critical attributes of learning communities. It is essential that mutual respect be exemplified by all participants. Everyone in the group is valued by all other members for what they can contribute to the group efforts as well as what they are becoming as individuals. Each participant is encouraged to make unique contributions that reflect his or her personal characteristics and idiosyncracies. The levels of interpersonal affection and respect lead all members to care about and protect each other from any unwarranted incursion that threatens either individual or group integrity or well-being.

Democratic discipline evolves in the process of learning community development. It is a hand-in-glove arrangement with perfect fit. Discipline approaches that have been developed apart from the instructional program are ordinarily incongruous with instruction. Commonly, so-called democratic approaches to discipline neither are truly democratic nor fit any particular instructional model. Many times this is due to the fact that almost all programs of instruction have few if any democratic elements. Because they are not truly democratic, associated discipline approaches cannot be carried out democratically.

In addition, nearly all discipline approaches that carry the label of being democratic fail in certain critical particulars to genuinely apply democratic principles. This incongruity is most evident in descriptions of recommended teachers' responses to student misbehavior. These strategies are usually punitive in their orientation, although the accompanying rhetoric may have a democratic sound. Thus, when disciplining their students, teachers may inform them that their misbehavior can lead to dire outcomes, suggesting that whatever consequences are imposed on them are of their own making, and thus logical and appropriate, when in reality they are punishments.

However, as already mentioned, this depends on how students interpret these actions. Ordinarily they see them as punitive and consequently may rebel or withdraw. Of course some can be compelled by such means to follow teachers' directives, but in reality such actions are far from democratic. It is true that many of these procedures are cloaked in democratic declamation, but most are imbued with control procedures that entice teachers to enact their own coercive inclinations.

Chapter One

Attributes of Learning Communities

Because discipline methods are commonly employed without regard to the nature of the instructional program, discipline and instruction are seen as independent processes and are often based on conflicting principles and practices. Thus, behaviorist approaches like Assertive Discipline or Behavior Modification may be implemented by teachers to control deviant behavior while at the same time providing instruction based on humanistic principles.

Democratic Discipline in Learning Communities is an approach in which the same principles apply to both discipline and instruction. In addition, when properly applied in learning communities, instruction provides a basis for greatly reducing the incidence of discipline problems. Students not only help to regulate their own learning, but work to prevent and eliminate discipline problems. When teachers properly implement learning communities, discipline problems virtually become negligible.

Learning communities are especially effective in helping students explore personally meaningful concepts and ideas as well as helping them learn how to solve complex problems and function successfully in democratic societies. Modern societies are very complex and hardly amenable to understanding without educational experiences specifically designed for this. In addition, many human experiences involve life in communities, and success there depends on having an understanding of community operations and the ability to successfully apply life skills.

Traditional schools are not designed for this purpose. They reflect the assumption that a common stock of information should be memorized that can then be used by anyone to live successfully in any particular environment. The complexity of society has increased drastically since the advent of greater social mobility and skyrocketing immigration. Living successfully, and even surviving, requires considerable skill, particularly in solving problems and knowledgeably relating to others.

Learning communities provide an unparalleled format for meaningful study and for preparing students to live successfully in democratic societies. Through participation in learning communities, children gain authentic experience in adjusting to and solving problems in the present as well as in preparing for the future. A good deal of human activity occurs in social situations that require far more skill than most children possess. Some of the necessary preparation for these activities evolves during unstructured social events, but much more is required for children to become adequately successful in working with others.

Unfortunately, traditional schools and the curricula imposed there have different goals and expectations. Thus, students are generally expected to do their own work so that their teachers can verify their level of competency in terms of the information they commit to memory. Most school learning requires students to sit quietly as they listen to lectures and engage in seatwork. Their learning is then evaluated through paper-and-pencil tests (Goodlad, 1984).

In traditional schooling students have relatively few opportunities for independent inquiry or significant academic involvement with other students, and rarely do they engage in extended learning wherein they produce high-quality products and reports. Hardly ever are they expected to teach their peers about the results of their research. In addition, their studies do not authentically represent the kind of human activity common in all walks of life and in all kinds of employment. In particular, traditional school learning does not prepare students for life in democratic communities. It is rare for them to become involved in school activities that are specifically designed to prepare them for life in the real world. The goals they are required to pursue, as well as the contexts in which these are pursued, are usually barren regarding current as well as future realities.

Faced with the common criticism of schools, policy makers have dictated changes in education that are based on strategies that have had little or no positive effect on learning. Current instruction in school is oriented toward standardized tests and is devoid of curricula as teachers ordinarily conceive it. Minimum standards have usually been mandated along with highly controlled management systems that emphasize supervision, evaluation, and penalties for noncompliance. There is almost no room for teachers to make decisions based on their own judgment and experience and the current reality of their classrooms.

Such mandates commonly imitate corporate management models, which do not really articulate with specific classroom requirements and operations. The market theories that are commonly applied to education have never been carefully evaluated in terms of school applications. These systems involve competition and rewards that generally fail to produce intended changes. Schools seem impervious to these initiatives. They may dictate changes in school structure, but they have little effect on the basic school purposes of teaching and learning (Sergiovanni, 2000).

Appropriate, deep changes require more local control and less interference from bureaucrats. All members of the local community, including teachers, parents, students, and administrators, need to become substantially involved, rather than leaving important educational decisions in the hands of bureaucratic entities (Hiatt & Diana, 2001). The greatest effectiveness occurs when students and their teachers are the most significant determiners of school curricula (Keefe & Jenkins, 2002).

Most changes in recent years have been initiated within the existing school structure, resulting in relatively few significant improvements. The fundamental changes that are needed consequently do not take place (Newman, 1998; Sergiovanni, 2000). The best indicator of a good school may well be the extent to which it reflects the needs and desires of parents, teachers, and students (Sergiovanni, 2000). For this to happen, a moral order must be created that binds students and teachers together. This requires that the driving force behind classroom operations be personal and interactive. Both teachers and their students must share in decision making about curriculum and instruction rather than being regulated by individuals outside the school.

With outside direction, the classroom organizational character erodes, creating many school dysfunctions, including excessive student disengagement and disruptiveness and low student performance (Sergiovanni, 2000). A balance must be struck between the influence of outside entities and classroom teachers. Otherwise, bureaucratic take-over ensues with the loss of the energizing influence of personal agency. The result is loss of authentic learning productivity.

THE NATURE OF LEARNING COMMUNITIES

In learning communities students become connected to learning purposes and to one another in terms of commitments rather than contracts. Contractual arrangements tend to be without personal care and involvement. Instead they are framed by legalistic obligations. However, members of learning communities become committed to each other through bonds of common values and ideas and become socially organized around relationships that are nurtured by independence (Blau & Scott, 1962).

Life in common organizations and life in democratic communities differ substantially. In many organizations, relationships are constructed for members by others and become codified into a system of hierarchies, roles, and role expectations. On the other hand, in learning communities, members create their social lives with others who have intentions and desires similar to their own. Instead of relying on external control, communities depend on group norms, purposes, and values, along with collegiality, caring, and thoughtful interdependence.

Once they are created, community ties effectively replace formal supervision and evaluation. There is no need for outsiders to coordinate what teachers and students do or how they work together. Instead of hierarchical control, leadership is shared between teachers and their students (Sergiovanni, 1992). In communities, students and teachers are empowered by a relationship between personal discretion and freedom and group commitment, obligations, and a felt sense of duty. Collegiality does not come from organizational arrangements forced on people but rather from connections members make to one another as a result of felt interdependence and mutual obligations.

To become effective, school communities must become purposeful. This involves acquiring several critical attributes. First, they must become caring communities where each individual is the recipient of altruistic love and where all members share a high level of commitment to common purposes. Second, all members must become committed to thinking and making well-reasoned inquiries regarding the world around them. Learning through inquiry becomes a way of life. Third, members must become committed to the development of personal expertise in the acts of both teaching and learning. Fourth, members must be tied together for their mutual benefit in the pursuit of common goals and exhibit responsible interdependence along with a sense of mutual obligation. Fifth, economic, religious, cultural, ethnic, family, and other differences must be brought together into a mutually respectful whole. Differences should be celebrated and used to expand perceptions and understandings. Sixth, a spirit of collective inquiry should be promoted in a search for solutions to problems that face the community (Sergiovanni, 1994).

Important Community Ingredients

Becoming a purposeful learning community involves common values. Values affect the way students think, feel, and behave. The values students select to guide their actions should be so significant that they permeate their life at school. Values should serve as guides through which students make sense of their lives together, find purposeful direction in their study, and make commitments to each other regarding courses of action. Common values provide students with a sense of security regarding social commitments and efforts they make to learn and be productive. They circumscribe the purposes with which students frame their world and give meaning to it.

In learning communities members develop a community of mind that binds them to a shared ideology. For example, caring for each other becomes unalterably valued. A caring community cannot exist unless caring is valued and unless norms are created that provide directions for caring, show its critical importance to all members, and manifest disapproval of non-caring attitudes and behavior. The culture of schools must arise from a network of shared ideologies consisting of coherent sets of beliefs that tie people together and provide an understanding of their involvement in terms of cause-and-effect relationships (Trice & Beryer, 1984). These ideologies constitute the means by which group members makes sense of their lives, find direction, and become committed to particular courses of action.

Ideologies shape the ways principals and teachers practice their craft and how students learn and behave. The meanings that evolve from these beliefs affirm that the actions of all members are purposeful and sensible. Because community values dictate how people think, feel, and behave, the values the group selects should be so significant that they permeate every aspect of the school and provide a sense of purposeful direction and satisfaction.

It is important that parents be involved in the formation of school ideology. This provides a framework within which teachers and parents can reach agreement on what the school emphasizes and wishes to accomplish. Once children realize that there is agreement between parents and the school, greater commitment can be built within the student body.

In creating a community, a conception must be established about what schools are for, actions and activities that are good for students, what makes sense about teaching and learning, and how everyone involved should live their lives together. Thus, a community of mind is developed. In this process, educators should leave plenty of room for each individual to shape his or her own destiny while being informed by the key values of the group.

Within a learning community certain assumptions must be held to in providing a vibrant, appropriate curriculum. First, it is assumed that children are inherently curious. They need to explore and manipulate real things that involve more than one sense. They must be involved in examining all aspects of the real world.

Second, children's behavior is usually purposeful. Ordinarily they search for patterns in terms of organizing new information in relation to previously held concepts. Incongruity between old patterns and new experiences stimulates questioning, observation, manipulation, and the potential for making applications in a variety of new situations. In managing instruction, teachers should try to maintain the right balance between novel and familiar experiences in order for students to acquire a meaningful understanding of what they confront and try to fathom. To do this, students need to explore their world without undue structure and without learning experiences based on excessive knowledge transmission.

Third, it is assumed that learning experiences gain power if they are part of conceptual wholes that students have conscientiously organized. The process of conceptualizing creates meaning, which drives children to learn more and to apply what they learn to their lives. When these efforts are directed toward problems that children recognize and wish to solve in order to improve their lives, there is considerable motivation to learn.

Fourth, when children are successful in their learning efforts, they acquire self-fulfillment and do not require external rewards and approval to be motivated. When children find meaning in what they learn, they become happy and involved.

Fifth, children have an intrinsic need for mastery over problems they confront. This is expressed in their efforts to search out significant patterns in life and reduce the uncertainty they feel about what they observe. When children discover that through their own efforts they are able to confront life's problems successfully, and acquire greater predictability regarding their actions, they achieve greater confidence in themselves and become increasingly more proficient in problem solving.

Sixth, play is not simply a diversion, it is an essential part of the learning process. When play is promoted, the learning environment is free from restrictions like teacher and peer evaluations and judgment. With play being employed, children are free to try out different styles of action and communication without being penalized when they make mistakes. Play thus provides a context within which teachers can observe their students and get a more accurate picture of them and their learning proclivities.

Seventh, children learn best through self-directed experiences with people, symbols, and things. These experiences can involve objects, events, processes, or relationships. This process is akin to the way in which adults confront the world and become involved in democratic communities. The critical importance of this disposition should not be underestimated. School is a particularly good environment in which to learn to properly apply this natural inclination.

Eighth, children inherently desire group involvement. Only in groups can their needs be fully satisfied. In this configuration they learn the give and take of successful group activity. School work should capitalize on this natural inclination.

Ninth, children come to understand symbolic information through concrete representation. They learn that real phenomena can be represented by such symbols as a spoken word, a gesture, a dramatic movement, a toy, a model, or a picture. Symbolism underlies the communication, recording, and coding of experiences that make it possible to think abstractly and properly understand knowledge and interact with others.

These assumptions apply regardless of children's background and previous school activities. It then becomes a matter of providing school experiences that are consistent with these assumptions. Learning communities provide the best learning configuration in which to accomplish this.

The Growth of a Community

As learning communities gradually develop, more of the activities in which students engage are compelled from within. They become less and less affected by the kind of outside influences that tend to distort the critical purposes to which group members have devoted themselves. When student learning becomes more self-directed it also becomes more self-sustaining. Students become eager, self-regulating participants in group learning and more willing to extend themselves to become responsible partners, bound to their colleagues and their teachers by reciprocal webs of moral obligation. Personal rights, discretion, and freedom become inextricably connected to the commitments, obligations, and duties they feel toward group members. There is a melding of personal desires with group duty and obligation. Learning communities are more productive when they become:

1. Reflective communities—where students and teachers come to understand their own strengths and weakness and use these understandings to improve personal as well as group learning.
2. Developmental communities—where students and teachers understand that group members are developmentally different. Each person has different rates of development along with different capacities in various intellectual areas.
3. Diverse communities—where the interests of both students and teachers are not only allowed expression, but also encouraged. These interests provide direction for curriculum construction, teaching, and evaluation.
4. Conversational communities—where community members are encouraged to engage in active discourse with each other and together make in-depth explorations of both interests and values.
5. Caring communities—where personal differences are not only accepted, but also celebrated because of the additional insights they produce. Community members actively look after the needs and interests of each other and promote their well-being, particularly when there is a potential for prejudice and bullying.
6. Responsible communities—where community members take their responsibilities seriously as members of the group. Each individual acquires a moral obligation to the group not only for the present, but also his or her future role as a citizen (Sergiovanni, 1999).

The Purpose of a Covenant in a Learning Community

Perhaps the most important process in forming learning communities is the
establishment of a covenant. The term *covenant* is befitting because it implies a sacred enterprise with an unusual degree of commitment (Sergiovanni, 1999). It stands for the creation of basic principles of operation that the
school will not compromise. The purposes and practices that spring from
well-conceived community deliberations are considered too important to ignore or abandon for less cogent intentions (Glickman, 1993).

A school covenant community consists of students, teachers, administrators, and parents who feel a strong sense of agreement and belonging. Most
particularly they come to think of the welfare of the learning community as
more important than any individual or subgroup. In noting this, it must be
recognized that the group has a supreme commitment to the welfare of each
individual.

Membership in the community inspires deep loyalty, compelling individuals to work together for the common good, while at the same time promoting the interests and capabilities of individuals. The group sincerely works to
help individuals acquire fulfillment within a collective configuration because
each individual's needs and aspirations can best be met within a community.
In a covenant community, members not only help each other work toward a
consensus of ideas and commitments, but also assist each other in making
self-fulfilling applications in their personal lives.

One of the problems faced in a commitment to individualism rather than
community is the view of people as being naturally independent and autonomous, self-serving and self-motivated, with concern above all else about
personal welfare. However, there is almost always a social context in which
choices must be made. This is what makes a covenant central to the well-
being of each individual. It recognizes the need for some form of common
good while still valuing independent thought and disagreement. Students
must realize that citizens in a democracy are in it together. Consequently they
must have a civic identity, not simply a private one. But within the social
structure all entities inside as well as outside the school must know how to
properly respond to each individual's deepest concerns (Beyer, 1998).

Community covenants are composed by everyone who participates in the
educational enterprise. These covenants are used as the basis for decision
making, as well as helping to establish school priorities regarding staff,
schedules, materials, assessment, the curriculum, staff development, and resource allocation (Allen, Rogers, Hensley, Glanton, & Livingston, 1999;
Glickman, 1993).

For the sake of clarification it is necessary to differentiate covenants from
contracts. Contracts usually contain agreements, with associated punishments for noncompliance. Ordinarily they specify acceptable minimums

rather than focusing on potentials. Covenants, on the other hand, employ the concept of maximums. In addition, they encourage community thinking and policy making (Qvortrup, 1997).

Most significantly, covenants exceed requirements expressed in contracts and initiate a variety of actions designed to nourish and sustain the community (Wickett, 2000). Thus, the orientation is toward growth rather than restriction. Learning communities fulfill covenant obligations for what Sergiovanni (1996) refers to as "sacred reasons" that are filled with collegiality, unity, and care. Interdependence of group members is based on genuine affection and reciprocal devotion to each other and their common purposes. These dependencies are not limiting nor debilitating, as are those based on extrinsic rewards and regulated by contracts, but are enlarging because they are reciprocal.

All members of the covenant internalize a pledge to help further the welfare of each group member and consequently that of the entire community. With contracts, participants interact in a legalized way, based on personal desires and obligations. Contracts tend to be fulfilled exactly with no effort to produce anything beyond the strict limits. Therefore, in meeting contract obligations nothing extra is given nor is the welfare of participants considered, let alone any effort given to provide various possible enhancements.

When learning communities have become properly developed, their purposes embrace the vision of leaders in and out of the classroom as well as a covenant shared by group members. The covenant furnishes the value pattern essential for exceptional learning effectiveness and a vision that exhibits the hopes and dreams, the needs and interests, of students, and the values and beliefs of everyone who has a stake in the school. Eventually the vision provides the image of the ideals for which the school exists.

The vision of the learning community drives the daily behavior of members toward community purposes (Brandt, 1992). The covenant is a binding and solemn agreement regarding what the learning community stands for, as well as the commitments made by members to each other. During the process of building consensus about purposes and beliefs, individuals are bound together around common themes, with a sense of mission and group ownership (Sergiovanni, 1990). It is unfortunate that research into present-day schooling reveals a near vacuum with respect to mission (Goodlad, 2000).

In creating a covenant community, questions can be raised regarding how the school can become a purposeful, caring, inquiring, and respectful community of learners. For example: How do children naturally learn? What kinds of learning activities are consistent with the way children actually learn? How can the school help children to engage in personally satisfying, meaningful learning? What kind of school experiences are most likely to prepare students to become persons of character in a democratic society?

What stimulates students to think deeply about the world and their place in it? What kinds of experiences help students to become more conscious of the needs of others and help them learn to balance their needs with those of their peers? What sorts of learning experiences help students to think deeply about concepts they confront and provide a way to build conceptual structures of knowledge that are consistent with information acquired by researchers over the years? What is it that students should come to know and do? How can students learn to work productively with adults?

Additional questions are also addressed: How can students become successfully articulated with the democratic communities in which they live? What should parents and the community at large do in order to become effectively involved in learning communities? What kinds of experiences help students learn to truly care about each other and about the school, and to focus on common purposes? How can obligations and commitments to common purposes be promoted without subverting individual interests and inclinations? How can accountability be enhanced in a learning community? How can all members of the learning community become skilled leaders as well as productive workers? What kinds of instruction help students acquire a sense of shared leadership (Sergiovanni, 1996)?

Creating a Covenant Community

Educators may wonder where to find learning communities that can be successfully imitated. Aside from acquiring basic principles, it is unwise to try to copy other learning communities. Each community should generate its own questions and answers regarding its structure and operations. Sufficient time and effort are necessary to determine good answers to some very critical but difficult questions. They are difficult because they most certainly involve digressions from traditional practices.

Predictably, difficulties and disagreements can be expected, yet consensus can and should be reached concerning issues that are central to the purposes and operations of the community. For example, considerations regarding how to evaluate student achievement, organize group learning, or share leadership likely require extensive discussion and clarification. In teaching and learning, children must be understood as inherently capable of high achievement, making efforts that can and should lead to academic success.

It should be understood that failure, as commonly allowed in school, never promotes student accomplishment. Instead, failure encourages perpetual deficiency, which comes about essentially because education is commonly defined in a way that promotes these consequences. Students should be filled with an understanding that they can learn from mistakes and that the errors they make in no way characterize them as students or as people. They are simply stepping-stones to greater understanding and higher achievement. Students should also learn that their greatest source of learning and understanding may come from their peers and their own investigations, not necessarily from the teacher or textbooks.

Ethical behavior should characterize relationships in the classroom. Ethics involve an understanding of what is morally right or wrong, conditions under which individuals are morally responsible for what they do, and what moral principles apply to community life. In addition, they indicate what traits or dispositions are morally good or bad and what outcomes are desirable from a moral point of view. With a proper ethical understanding, children are able to make assessments of various behaviors and social interactions.

It is important that moral considerations and ethical standards be drawn from all members of the learning community. They should never be coercively or arbitrarily imposed. In forming community standards that are sanctioned by the group, it is essential that they not be mechanistically restrictive, but should be considered as guidelines with sufficient flexibility to accommodate the requisite decision-making autonomy necessary for each individual to acquire a sense of personal empowerment to go along with the caring relationships that are so critical to personal satisfaction (Coombe, 1999).

Members of a learning community should always consider knowledge as partial and somewhat fallible. Thus, what is learned should be considered tentative as group members engage in investigations. What is learned should be enriched by sharing meanings and interpretations. Participants should anticipate that during discussions they may decide to change their minds or modify their understandings.

In addition, the learning agenda should usually involve experiences that are intrinsically human, with inquiry being directed toward questions which are important to students as individuals and as social beings. For this reason, it is wise for the inquiry-based curriculum to consist of comprehensive projects that are related to strategic questions that students have about the world in which they live.

Often children's understanding is greatly enhanced by learning that involves a historical perspective. Many problems are best viewed in terms of their connections to events of the past. For example, current problems in the world usually have historical connections that, if ignored, spawn misunderstanding and poor decision making. Thus, seeing religion as the source of many world problems helps learners predict what might happen in future events and perhaps help them avert problems in their personal and social lives that typically repeat themselves.

Also, in the area of science, if students comprehend how science has evolved, they will be better equipped to understand that science is not a static understanding of basic concepts that currently exist. Rather, they will appreciate how science concepts have changed over time and how true learning in science involves an inquiry-oriented approach to understanding and an ever-ready willingness to make new interpretations and applications.

There are plenty of examples of failure to accept new information and interpretations of natural phenomena. Always they show how an unwillingness to entertain new ideas holds up the advance of scientific knowledge, to the detriment of humanity. Thus, it is important that school learning be continuously related to students' everyday lives in order to capitalize on their interests, provide them with a way to make sense of current experiences relative to the past, and enable them to make insightful decisions regarding matters especially important to them, which takes into account that much knowledge is temporary and changeable (Starratt, 1996).

ATTRIBUTES OF LEARNERS IN AUTHENTIC LEARNING COMMUNITIES

School communities share a set of attributes that help them become places where students can achieve success, along with a sense of acceptance and worth. These include respect, caring, inclusiveness, trust, empowerment, and commitment (Raywid, 1993).

Respect exists when students and teachers have authentic regard for each other as unique persons. Current classrooms are commonly made up of diverse populations with a potential for misunderstanding and conflict. Often individuals ascribe negative attributes to anyone different from themselves. This, of course, is due to personal insecurities, along with being indoctrinated by prejudiced individuals. When prejudice is perpetuated, children become suspicious of each other and create various means to differentiate themselves from others and to criticize and attack them because they are different.

However, in learning communities there is no room for negative stereotypes regarding human attributes and capacities. As already indicated, differences are to be celebrated, not used as a basis for discrimination. In reality, when students become open to others who are different, they increase their chances of acquiring a far better understanding of the world. When they caringly interact with their peers, they are able to gather more insights and achieve an understanding that far exceeds that which is circumscribed by prejudice and lack of respect.

Caring is more explicitly delineated and proactive than respect. Caring individuals reach out in an attempt to initiate positive interactions with others and to promote affirming relationships. Caring people initiate acts of kindness in an effort to relieve the discomfort experienced by associates and to provide support. They conscientiously anticipate opportunities for relieving others' discomfort and easing their burdens. Caring students acquire a sense of satisfaction in supporting the learning of their peers. They are character-ized as willing to sacrifice personal desires in order to ensure their peers receive their help and achieve success.

In setting aside personal desires in favor of helping others, students as-cend to a much more advanced level of community life. Herein is the way in which individual hopes and desires can be articulated with the needs of the group. Setting aside personal interests in favor of helping peers not only provides needed assistance, it also advances the group agenda as well as contributing to the growth of the sacrificing individual and ensuring that his or her personal needs are satisfied more fully than if they were more self-focused in their efforts. Students with a heightened sense of care feel that to do deliberate harm to another human being is unthinkable (Noddings, 2002).

Inclusiveness defines the way in which group members work to ensure that everyone is drawn into a whole range of interactions and activities avail-able throughout the school. It includes an assurance that no one will ever be left out. Thus, students learn to look out for one another, anticipating the possibility that some group members may be left out of various activities, but trying to make certain that this never happens. Students help to ensure that there are no physical or psychological issues, or levels of achievement, that are allowed to segregate them from their peers. There are no cliques. Bias is unacceptable regarding levels of achievement, religion, gender, race, culture, economic levels, or any other characteristic.

Students eventually learn ways of deliberately integrating all group mem-bers and helping to provide for the greatest possible diversity. In the process, everyone is able to acquire a broader conception of the world and obtain a better idea regarding how to successfully interact in the complex world in which they live. Discrimination becomes nonexistent in a properly run learn-ing community. Because students and teachers share a common culture, with attendant values and assumptions about conduct and expectations, conflict is greatly reduced and unity prevails rather than an environment supporting a "survival of the fittest" mentality, as is often the case in traditional schools.

Learning communities cannot function without considerable trust. When trust is absent, significant interactions between community members are greatly limited. Authentic interactions in learning communities depend on unqualified trust in order for participants to willingly make personal disclo-sures, work energetically with others in promoting more meaningful relation-ships, and supporting learning excellence for all. Students must be assured that the information they disclose will never be inappropriately used.

It has become fairly common for groups of students to "trash" fellow students they wish to exclude from cliques they form. They spread rumors, exclude targeted individuals from the social group, and withdraw friendship and acceptance. They engage in behaviors designed to significantly damage another child's reputation, limit friendship, stimulate negative feelings, and destroy the person's self-worth (Espelage, Mebane, & Swearer, 2004).

Often false, derogatory information is passed around using current technology. This is called cyber-bullying. This is done through e-mails, text messaging, social networking sites, chat rooms, blogs, and websites (Kowalski, Limber, & Agatston, 2008). Some cliques even stoop to transmitting embarrassing images of the targeted student, acquired in school shower rooms, to one another on their cell phones. Eventually the marked student is exposed to the same images and suffers the associated humiliation (Keith & Martin, 2005). This kind of relational aggression has no place in schools and is specifically combated in learning communities.

Children learn the complex skills and dispositions of adulthood though close association with adults who consistently exhibit moral behavior, are knowledgeable regarding students' needs and dispositions, and have a valid understanding of learning processes. When children are involved in trusting relationships with friends and teachers they aren't afraid to take risks, make mistakes, or "do something dumb." Children learn best when the very idea that some activity is risky in terms of their relationships hasn't even occurred to them (Meier, 2002).

In learning communities students as well as teachers are able to secure an authentic sense of empowerment because they know that they are listened to carefully and taken seriously during group interactions. They have a guarantee that community members will not intentionally hurt their feelings, and have the added assurance that this protection will even extend beyond the classroom.

In traditional schools, it is common practice to withhold decision-making power from students. They are rarely consulted regarding their opinions, particularly about what they learn and how they are evaluated. They are thus left with the impression that their point of view is not respected even when they may have valid input to give. Because of this disenfranchisement, students tend to withdraw. Those in charge ordinarily do not respect the opinions and preferences of students because they are considered too immature, inexperienced, and self-serving.

Educators often fail to recognize the positive influence student empowerment can have. When students are respected and taken seriously, their interest in school increases. They experience increased vigor for learning and become more fully committed. All this occurs along with students acquiring a greater sense of ownership. Student ownership is probably the greatest learning motivator available to teachers.

Without commitment, schools fail to promote strong interpersonal attachments and are unable to energize the work in which community members engage. Without a sense of connection and commitment to the group enterprise, members find little reason to internalize the goals and values of the school. Children simply refuse to take on such attachments and obligations when they do not feel empowered through taking on an authentic role in decision making regarding classroom procedures. Teachers experience the same thing when their decision-making role is unnecessarily restricted. When all members of the learning community are properly enabled, they obtain the necessary commitment to work conscientiously and achieve the best results possible for themselves and all others concerned.

All of the above attributes of authentic communities are interrelated. Thus, commitment does not emerge without participants being empowered, and empowerment is impossible without sufficient trust. In addition, until all community members are respected and sense that they are cared for and valued unconditionally, trust will fail to unfold. All of these factors are needed in an integrated way in order for an authentic community to grow. This requires schools that are committed to decentralizing their operations and trusting both teacher and student decision making. When schools are run bureaucratically, none of these empowering factors materialize (Hiatt & Diana, 2001). The result of this failure can be witnessed in a plethora of school deficits that are increasingly referred to in educational research and the popular press.

STAGES IN THE DEVELOPMENT OF LEARNING COMMUNITIES

In building communities, various human attributes and inclinations must be taken into account. As already mentioned each learning community is unique. There should be no effort to imitate any other group. Because of the uniqueness of each learning community, in addition to the reality of differences between members, community building goes through developmental stages. Peck (1987) has identified four transition stages in community growth: the pseudo-community stage, chaos stage, emptiness stage, and community stage.

Pseudo-Community Stage

The first stage is the pseudo-community stage. During this time members attempt to be extremely pleasant with each other and avoid all disagreements. Teachers should be wary of such conditions in the beginning. Children do in fact have different ideologies and theologies that inherently conflict with each other. Perhaps children are more likely than adults to express themselves honestly on points of disagreement, but many may hide their true feelings in an effort to be courteous and avoid an attack by their peers. Many have been taught to behave in such a way without realizing that true communities are conflict resolving by nature, rather than conflict avoiding as is true of pseudo-communities.

Teachers should make their students beware of becoming an instant community. Community building requires time as well as effort and sacrifice. It does not help for members to come together with the pretense of civility and still harbor disagreements with their peers and negative feelings. Some of these tendencies for dealing with potential conflict are unconscious and are carried out by individuals telling little white lies in an attempt to appear loving, or withholding some of the truth about themselves and their feelings in order to avoid negative implications about who and what they are.

Pseudo-communities fail to acknowledge individual differences by ignoring them. Many may be so accustomed to being well-mannered that they deploy their good manners without even thinking about the implications of such behavior in building an authentic community composed of individuals with differences who can work successfully with one another because they have learned to appreciate differences as helping to enlarge their own understanding of the world.

In authentic communities conflicting ideas are not looked upon as offence producing. They are differences of opinion that are to be used for comparison and advancing understanding. If a group member does or says something that is offensive, annoying, or irritating, it is not helpful to simply pretend as if nothing has happened or act as though you are not bothered in the least. Such actions may appear to help produce a smoothly functioning group, but they also suppress individuality, intimacy, and honesty, which are critical ingredients of a properly functioning learning community.

When individual differences are denied, as they are in pseudo-communities, the group fails to entertain input that would lead to better understanding and the appropriate modification of views held by the members. What ought to be examined is kept obscured when it could be responsible for helping members acknowledge their differences and at the same time learn to appreciate them. When pseudo-communities prevail, no such acknowledgments take place. Each individual continues to espouse his or her same narrow views.

Members of pseudo-communities tend to speak in generalities. They make blanket statements as if they represent universal truth. Others, whose beliefs differ from those expressed, tend to avoid conflict by keeping their disagreements to themselves. They may even nod in agreement in an effort to appear agreeable. Some people engage in such tactics for the sake of avoiding challenges, even when they recognize that speaking in generalities destroys genuine communication.

In addition to creating an illusion, people who promote the agenda of pseudo-communities forfeit personal integrity. They in fact live a lie. Teachers who witness groups of students engage in pseudo-community maneuvers should step in and help them engage in more productive interactions. For example, suppose a student named John says in a social studies class, "The President of the United States should never be criticized." The teacher, knowing that there may be differences of opinion on the issue, may say, "John, you are making a generalization. Let's look at the ways other people may feel. What if you said, 'I have learned that people should be sure they have their facts straight when they criticize the President of the United States?'" Such clarifying remarks help clear the way for other class members to present their views without fearing reprisal. The teacher could also just invite other students who have a different point of view to respond before making any reaction.

Chaos Stage

The second stage identified by Peck in community development is chaos. This aspect of creating a community centers around well-intentioned but misguided attempts by individuals to heal disagreements and convert others to their way of thinking. For example, after an uneasy silence during a discussion about religion and evolution, a member may say, "Well, I still believe God created the earth in six days."

A second member may respond by saying, "I used to believe that way until I visited a quarry and observed the different levels of fossilized animals there. They became more complex the further up the strata of the earth we looked."

"I've seen that," the first member answers, "but that doesn't change my mind. God could have made it look that way. Besides if you don't have God in your life, it's really empty. Accepting evolution requires you deny God's existence."

"I've tried to resolve this issue," says a third member. "I don't think you have to deny God to believe in evolution."

The first member responds, "You're just kidding yourself. That is the basic premise of evolution. It is concluded that it all happened by chance."

"I've heard that argument made," responds a fourth member. "I figure God simply used the process of evolution, but he directed everything."

"How can you say that," replies the first student. "I just can't believe that."

"Well, what you believe just isn't true," says a fifth member.

"You evolutionists just make me so angry," says the first member. "You don't know what you're talking about. You just create all this nonsense out of your heads. At least we have the Bible."

"You can't just believe in the Bible," indicates the third member. "There are a lot of things that are claimed to be miracles that just happened naturally. I've heard some investigators say that."

"You just don't know what you're talking about," the first member says. "The least we can do is believe in the Bible. It's been around for thousands of years."

"You're the one that's way off track," responds the fifth member. "How can you just accept the Bible because it is so old."

People resist changing their ideas. Consequently, converters try hard to get them to change their minds. This only causes the individuals being attacked to become angry and all the more resistant. The result is chaos. This stage is not to be avoided. It is an essential part of the community development process. Instead of differences being hidden, as is the case during the pseudo-community stage, in chaos they are brought out in the open. Now instead of group members trying to hide or ignore opposing viewpoints, they attempt to annihilate them. Generally there is no attempt to heal out of love, but rather to win an argument. Members fight over whose ideas should prevail.

Even though the chaos stage is defined as a time of struggle regarding what to accept as group norms, this is not the true essence of this process. Similar struggles occur in a fully mature community. Often discussions become heated, but they are oriented toward achieving consensus rather than asserting ones' own views and subverting those of other group members. In the chaos stage, people dispute each other with no intention of achieving agreement. Consequently productivity is nil.

During chaos, students may even attack their teacher, blaming him or her for the lack of agreement and low success. Members likely believe that chaos could and should have been avoided had proper leadership been employed. This may result in students trying to take over leadership. Their plea ordinarily is to impose some kind of organization on the group. This should be resisted.

Though organization appears to be the way out of chaos, organization and community are incompatible. Organization ordinarily embodies excessive structure, which has the effect of hamstringing the flow of community operations. Instead, creativity and individual responsibility should be encouraged. Mature communities have to be able to risk the lack of structure in order to achieve their purposes. There are ebbs and flows in community work that accommodate the agency of members as they work to investigate various intriguing phenomena. At the same time group cohesiveness is promoted. There is a flexible relationship between the community covenants and individually oriented motivations.

Resolution of chaos is not easy. Because it is usually both unproductive and unpleasant, it may appear to members that community building has irretrievably degenerated, and that good relations and productivity have become unreachable. This state of affairs, however, is preferable to retaining a pseudo-community. At least during chaos, issues are being confronted openly. Conflict is preferable to pretending that it doesn't exist. It may be painful, but it is a necessary beginning to the process of resolution.

Eventually members will conclude that they need to move beyond conflict, embrace the virtue of celebrating the vibrant context out of which various views can become a part of group deliberations, and learn to accept cultural differences as essential elements for a valid understanding of society. Group members should conclude that such a state of affairs provides a positive, legitimate representation of life and the best framework in which to accomplish their critically important agendas. This is far better than hiding behind a facade of lies and distortions and believing there is no reason to advance beyond it.

Emptiness Stage

Emptiness is the third stage of community development. When the group perpetually engages in squabbling and getting nowhere, they may come to believe that a more strict organization is the answer. However, as stated earlier, organization is an enemy of community. Despite the fact that wrangling with each other is likely to continue despite suggestions for imposing organizational restrictions, the teacher should step in and suggest that they move to the stage of emptiness.

In doing this, teachers must help students understand that emptiness is very difficult, but also the most crucial stage of community development. It constitutes a bridge between chaos and mature communities and involves emptying themselves of barriers to communication. They need to recognize the feelings, assumptions, ideas, and motives that have filled their minds and made them impervious to the views and values of others. Before people can be prepared to participate in genuine community experiences, they must empty themselves of common barriers to communication. According to Peck (1987), these include (1) expectations and preconceptions; (2) prejudices; (3) ideology, theology, and solutions; (4) the need to heal, convert, fix, or solve; and (5) the need to control.

Expectations and Preconceptions

For most people, community building is an adventure into the unknown. Efforts to engage in the emptiness process are particularly unnerving. In response to their insecurities, students are likely to make the experience conform to their expectations. Ordinarily this response is a pernicious one. It is not until participants are able to clear themselves of expectations and stop trying to fit their relationships with others into a preconceived pattern that it is possible to really listen attentively and become open to experience. Participants must learn to trust themselves and others as they enter into unfamiliar social territory and open themselves up to learn rather than expecting everything that transpires to fit a particular mold.

Prejudices

Prejudice is often employed as if the individual was unconscious of it and its implications. Ordinarily it is a judgmental impression or expression about someone that is devoid of any previous experience or knowledge about them. We might believe, for example, that a person looks like a nerd, only to find out later that this is not true. Sometimes people assume prejudicial things about others with whom they have had only brief, limited experiences.

Most people seem unaware of personal prejudices and many times attempt to discover actions by others that confirm their false conceptions. For example, I know of an individual who was thought by his department chairman to be uncooperative. Through the years this resulted in the department chairman depriving the individual of funding and opportunities of various kinds. On one occasion the department chairman made a request of all individuals in the department to perform some tasks that most found to be vexing and time consuming. Only the individual who the department chairman prejudged as uncooperative completed the tasks.

Then looking back, the department chairman realized that he could not recall even one instance in which the so-called uncooperative person failed to cooperate completely with what was expected. He realized, too late, that his first prejudiced conception of the person was completely erroneous. Ironically, he never took the time to check out his misconceptions before restricting opportunities for this person, while giving various advantages to less-cooperative department members. In community building, sufficient time and appropriate instruction and experiences must be provided in order to give all participants an opportunity to empty themselves of prejudice.

Ideology, Theology, and Solutions

Nearly everyone believes that what they think is absolutely true. Often people draw these conclusions without any particular evidence. When they look upon the activities of others, they often judge them to be wrong simply because they believe they know the only right way. This inclination appears to be inherent in humans. Interestingly, what is in our minds is unique to us. No one else has an identical conception of the world.

When someone else expresses an idea that is in conflict with our understanding, we usually judge it to be in error. It is hard to accept the possibility that our own thinking may be incorrect. There is too much at stake. For example, we may fear being deprived of others' respect along with facing a loss of personal security if we make statements that turn out to be false. If this happens, we then try to defend our views by pointing out the errors in the opinions of others.

To overcome this problem, community members need to abandon ideological and theological rigidities that they believe everyone else must accept. This doesn't mean that we should abandon our beliefs. Rather, it refers to the propriety of accepting the potential validity of others' beliefs and ideas. They may not necessarily be true, but we should not assume that there is only one way to think about things and only one correct conception of the world.

Also, we should not categorically forsake our personal sentiments and understandings simply for the sake of avoiding conflict. As students learn to empty themselves of constraining ideologies and theologies, their interpersonal interactions predictably reflect greater sensitivity to others' ideas and embrace more social compatibility with them. They become inclined to listen patiently and inquisitively to the expressions of their peers about their beliefs without finding them threatening to their own. They are not only comfortable in allowing the expressions of different opinions, but also are intrinsically interested in how these compare with personal views. In the process, they are able to obtain a fuller view of things. For example, members may have different opinions about God, which initially they voraciously defend. In the end they may not have changed their views of deity, but now converse about different views of God curiously, not defensively.

The Need to Heal, Convert, Fix, or Solve

During the chaos stage when members try to change others' ideas, they are convinced they are acting in a loving way. It is later a surprise for them to learn that they have not been. Earlier they have concluded that in helping someone else obtain a "correct view of things" the individual is relieved to finally see the light. It is thought that these recipients of the "truth" should be full of gratitude when, in fact, they react by fighting back aggressively. Of course, almost all of the attempts to convert and heal others regarding what we judge to be their inappropriate views and behavior are not only naive and ineffective but also self-centered and self-serving. The cures we offer rarely induce others to acknowledge the presumed error of their ways. And it is unlikely that they will simply accept our efforts to "set them straight" and thus improve their lives.

Calling someone's theology or ideology into question is more likely to promote discomfort and encourage misunderstanding and discord. If people believe they are successful in converting others to their way of thinking, they usually conclude that this is further proof of the virtue of their beliefs, which influences them to believe in their superiority. Learning communities are far better served when members extend themselves and attempt to understand others as they really are and purge themselves of any inclination to solve others' problems or try to make them change ideas judged to be in error.

During community building, members eventually must conclude that their desire to convert others and solve their problems as they believe they should is a self-centered desire for personal comfort and a quest for control. In the beginning, they suppose good will come from criticizing others' beliefs. Members believe it is necessary to convince others that they know a better way. It is assumed that the person will change his or her opinions and be grateful for being set straight. However, this is rarely the case.

Eventually it will dawn on the people seeking to alter the thinking of their associates that it is better to appreciate and celebrate the differences between themselves and their peers. To accomplish this, teachers have to remind their students that the purpose of being together is to form a learning community, not to vehemently assert personal views. They must empty themselves of the desire to promote their own proposals, ideas, and personal beliefs and begin to become better acquainted with associates and learn to appreciate their ideologies and theologies.

The Need to Control

The desire to control is perhaps the most predominant human attribute. Having control helps us satisfy all our needs in the way we wish. The most manifest conflict between people comes about through maneuvers to control others while remaining free of their control. Teachers have to be particularly careful not to assert too much control over their students. This is a difficult thing to do because they have been given the responsibility to teach, and if their efforts fail they are held responsible. This simply adds to teachers' inclinations to control excessively and consequently thwarts community building.

Paradoxically, teachers must learn to sit back and wait for progress to be made, all the while avoiding the temptation to manipulate the class to get things moving. To accomplish this, teachers must abandon the fear of failure. In essence, teachers must be willing to accept failure before they can really help learning communities properly develop. Students likewise must be encouraged to give up their fears. For example, some may find it difficult to abandon their usual orientation of working for grades instead of learning for intrinsic reasons. Others may need to shed their need for parents' approval regarding school accomplishments.

Students, no doubt, will see the process of giving up many of their impediments as a sacrifice. Teachers must help them see that what they give up actually has been standing in their way and keeping them from properly relating to others and learning. They must acknowledge that even though abandoning the fears to which they have become accustomed leaves them with a feeling of emptiness or annihilation, they will eventually experience a "rebirth."

This renewal has the power to carry them far beyond the encumbrances that have characterized their previous lifestyle. Group support is critical during this process. Members learn that there are struggles in life that can be overcome through the sustaining influence of friends, and that reciprocal support helps sustain others and consequently the group. The thing that must be resisted is the temptation to flee back to a pseudo-community stance.

Community

Community is the final stage. At this point the class gets on with the task at hand—the process of learning. Because the group has eliminated the need to criticize and compete with each other, learning tasks naturally arise and interests are followed with considerable vigor. Because a sense of care has emerged, there is a much greater adherence to a spirit of cooperation. Students find themselves looking after each other's interests and delving into very intriguing and useful learning projects in great depth. Because there is no concern about grades, learning takes on its own impetus. Students are driven intrinsically to learn and solve problems and to understand their world profoundly.

In the real world of learning communities, good teachers allow students to pursue credible personal interests. Although students may initially engage in a particular learning project, they should be allowed and even encouraged, as they clarify their aims during the learning process, to modify their learning strategies and even the nature of their plan when appropriate.

It is often difficult to nail down specific problem-solving undertakings or conceptual understandings in advance. Often more promising courses of action do not occur to the group in advance, but rather emerge as learning progresses. The outcomes of this kind of learning are unanticipated but nonetheless are to be highly valued. This is so because students not only acquire bonafide conceptual knowledge, they also benefit from a learning process that empowers them and helps them secure ownership and consequent learning motivation.

In addition, when their learning has a problem-solving orientation, they not only learn to recognize problems, but also become skilled in devising means for solving them. They discover that problem solving is a valid way to deal with the present and prepare for the future, and they come to understand that obtaining critical knowledge is essential to this process. Finally, they not only learn how to formulate caring relationships, they also find out that such experiences prepare them to work successfully with others and to more fully satisfy their needs (Peck, 1987).

ASSESSMENT IN LEARNING COMMUNITIES

Comparative student assessments are avoided in learning communities. Not only do they fail to produce all the information that is essential in truly understanding the results as well as the process of schooling, they also interfere with the learning process and create significant personal problems for many students. The rationale for employing traditional assessments in schools is tenuous compared to the justification ordinarily given for using other means to evaluate school operations.

The only defense ordinarily presented in support of common tests and grades is that they are a simple way to determine which students should be permitted to attend college, along with providing parents with information regarding their children's relative standing in their classes. These justifications fail to hold up when compared to the potential detriment of tests and grades and their inherent inability to satisfy validity requirements. Evaluation in learning communities is designed to be more comprehensive and more valid in terms of learning, as well as less hostile to students.

A focus on excellence is one significant difference between traditional testing and assessment in learning communities. Thus, traditional testing focuses on comparisons and features the normal curve, which deals primarily with the distribution of grades rather than excellence. Minimum standards are an essential part of traditional evaluation. These standards are below the capabilities of some students. Many students who could exceed minimum standards fail to do so because, given the nature of schooling, they see no reason to do it.

It is important to realize that in learning communities, excellence is variously defined depending on purposes. If students desire to evaluate performances relative to the world of work, one set of standards may apply. If college entrance is being pursued, another set of standards may be appropriate. Most students at least wish to acquire living skills, and excellence in this area may depend on specific aspects of students' aspirations. Consequently, considerable flexibility is needed. For example, one student may look upon art as a potential occupation, another as a field to teach, a third as a possible hobby, and a fourth as something to appreciate.

Not only does evaluation in learning communities focus on student achievement, as illustrated in their portfolios, assessments are also made of a variety of considerations that are not ordinarily examined in traditional appraisals. The following are examples of concerns in learning communities that are assessed that are ordinarily overlooked in traditional evaluations:

- The degree to which the needs of all students are met.
- The degree to which students achieve their defined level of excellence.

- The effectiveness of both adult and student leadership.
- The effectiveness of student cooperation.
- The degree of flexibility supported in the learning groups, and its effectiveness in providing students ample opportunities to pursue personal learning desires.
- The extent to which learning community members feel free to express themselves.
- The accessibility of materials that are used by students to learn and conduct research.
- The quality of social skills students acquire.
- The degree to which group learning is consistent with the covenant and associated group values.
- The level of teacher effectiveness in carrying out his or her role.
- The intellectual development of students.
- The quality of the research projects students pursue.
- The degree of excellence with which students conduct their research.
- The quality of the reports students write regarding their research.
- The level of skill students attain in evaluating their own achievements.
- The level of care with which students interact with each other.
- The extent to which students develop and practice essential life skills.
- The extent to which student portfolios accurately represent their accomplishments.
- The effectiveness of school administrators in supporting the learning community.
- The extent to which parents are meaningfully involved in the learning community.
- The degree to which students acquire a sophisticated understanding of the important knowledge obtained by scholars and others over time.
- The degree to which students are prepared for life in democratic communities outside the school.
- The validity of students' assessment of their own work.

Obviously these evaluation criteria go far beyond those ordinarily applied in traditional evaluation and are capable of supplying much more insight regarding the nature and effectiveness of instruction. Their focus is on carefully determining the extent to which critical educational purposes are achieved, rather than simply sorting students for college. They provide the means for examining a broad range of learning issues and allow for the purposes of all students to be considered. Thus, they take into account the various abilities and interests of students and help them trace their progress.

   The nature of evaluation that takes place in learning communities provides a way to ascertain the kind of support needed regarding students' unique desires and also the way in which each individual can gain the most from his or her associations in the group. Such considerations do not arise in traditional testing, whereas in learning communities they are considered absolutely essential.

With data regarding each student in a learning community routinely being addressed, teachers are armed with information needed to help each individual realize his or her true potential while being involved in learning activities that are truly educational and fulfilling. Obviously the teachers' role is not one of presenting information. Rather they take the data they receive from various evaluation measures and use it to improve student learning and ensure that all educational purposes are fully satisfied.

Chapter Two

Authentic Fulfillment of Student Needs

One of the schools' most critical responsibilities is to help students satisfy their needs.

In learning communities, this is a central task of teachers. However, it would be very unusual for traditional schools to focus much on satisfying the needs of students. Instead schools are nearly exclusively dedicated to transmitting information and determining students' ability to retrieve these facts, thus implicitly assuming that helping students acquire memorized knowledge is their sole responsibility. It is also presumed that transmitting knowledge adequately addresses children's need to achieve intellectual competence and learn how to get along in the adult world.

There seems to be no disagreement among educational theorists that the need for intellectual competence is real, although schools rarely promote it (Brendtro, Brokenleg, & Van Brockern, 1990; Coopersmith, 1967; Glasser, 1998; Kohn, 1993b.) Instead, children are confronted with what they believe is a plethora of meaningless facts, and it is commonplace for them to question whether or not intellectual competence is really the object of the education they receive.

Many of the problems students encounter in school stem from the mismatch between their authentic needs and what they experience there (Darling-Hammond, 1997). The depersonalized, punitive, rote-learning ambience which schools generally provide fails to meet children's needs for affiliation, autonomy, and cognitive challenges (Kohn, 1999).

Confronted with student objections and lack of success in school, critics often suggest that reforms should be made that involve a return to the basics of traditional curricula with their emphasis on acquiring factual information. This assumes that focusing even more on memorizing facts will solve school problems. However, the traditional schooling that the critics so highly value never provides an adequate education for anyone (Noddings, 2002). There is no evidence that a traditional education really prepares students for what they must do in the real world (Merrow, 2001). In fact, many employers lament the fact that graduating students lack the necessary skills to function success-fully on the job (Gose, 1997). They not only lack professional preparation, but also intellectual capabilities, appropriate attitudes, and character.

With greater emphasis on information accumulation, less time can be devoted to students' intellectual and moral development. For intellectual development to occur, students must be involved in inquiry investigations and problem solving. To promote moral development teachers must make this a central aspect of the curriculum and be more explicit moral examples themselves. They must provide a genuine caring environment in which stu-dents can also become caring, moral people (Fenstermacher, 1990; Meier, 2002; Noddings, 2002).

It must be admitted that some needs of a few students are addressed in the extracurricular program. However, these activities are not routinely scruti-nized to determine if the participating students all have need-satisfying expe-riences. In addition, many of these activities are not available to all students, for example athletics, debate, choir, plays, operettas, and the like. Because only a few of the more talented students can participate in these activities, an elitist attitude is often created among participants. The result is for self-concept to be framed either positively or negatively depending on whether or not students participate. Boys in particular receive accolades from their peers for their success in sports.

However, those who do not qualify to participate may experience deni-grating interactions with their peers because of not being athletically capable or inclined. Interestingly, athletic prowess may promote the self-concept of some students, but for many it provides troublesome ego-development (Kohn, 1992). Cliques are the usual outgrowths of exclusive activities. Some students are left unfulfilled because not only are they not allowed to partici-pate and receive a potential boost in self-concept, but they also may suffer denigrating remarks from others, which this state of affairs encourages.

The scenario for girls may be different, but they are exposed to the same hazards as boys as they try to substantiate their worthiness with their peers. So extracurricular activities fail to provide empowerment for all students and may actually be detrimental to some. In any case, schools usually fail to deliberately promote the development of the character attributes, either in various academic courses or in the extracurricular program, that are usually found in most descriptions of schooling purposes.

Other critical needs also fail to be fulfilled in the normal operations of most schools, including affiliation, acceptance, belonging, autonomy, and power, along with the development of valuable character traits. Teachers should not underestimate the importance students attach to satisfying their needs. They are not always consciously aware of all the needs they are pursuing, but their behavior, both good and bad, is primarily designed to gratify these needs.

BASIC STUDENT NEEDS

There is remarkable agreement among theorists regarding human needs. Of course, some small differences are present, and sometimes different words are used to describe similar concepts, but under careful scrutiny they reveal conspicuous similarities. In addition, most agree that satisfying needs is essential to living effectively in the school environment (Brendtro, Brokenleg, & Van Brockern, 1990; Coopersmith, 1967; Glasser, 1998; Kohn, 1993b).

The failure of teachers to understand the needs of youth is a major reason for so much unproductive, disruptive student behavior. In school, children face significant challenges in both meeting teachers' expectations and fulfilling their own needs, especially when these are contradictory. Because of their strategic position, educators routinely determine whether or not their students will be successful.

Wise teachers not only supply an appropriate need-fulfilling environment, they also protect children from the predictable thwarting of need fulfillment encountered in various school circumstances. It is insightful to recognize that most human behavior involves an effort to achieve personal needs (Glasser, 1998).

Unfortunately, some students give up their quest for need gratification when it becomes evident it is not possible in the schools. Others engage in aberrant conduct in an effort to gratify themselves no matter what. These attempts are usually irrational and often personally and socially detrimental. For example, why would students become so disruptive that they destroy any possibility of achieving positive attention and approval from their teachers and peers? Yet many students risk the hope of fulfilling their quest for approval when they attack others in the classroom venomously in an effort to satisfy their need to control. Their actions can hardly achieve the acceptance they pursue even from the most conscientious friends and teachers. The fact that teachers tend not to genuinely care for contentious youth makes their deviant crusade for attention exceedingly difficult to endure and respond to appropriately. Obviously students must learn how to satisfy their needs in socially acceptable ways (Glasser, 1990).

The Need for Love, Acceptance, and Belonging

The need for unconditional love and acceptance and belonging to social groups is a particularly potent one. Humans need to be accepted despite their personal idiosyncracies. Many times insignificant differences are used to create cliques and isolate students who do not have all the requisite characteristics. Ordinarily these identifying characteristics hold little credence in the real world, but in the artificial social world of the school they can be powerful deterrents to acceptance and care by peers.

In the struggle for personal identity, students increasingly isolate themselves according to certain defined characteristics and reject peers who don't possess these traits. It seems that to achieve a satisfactory sense of significance they find it necessary to belittle others. Along with rejection, outsiders are often subjected to various kinds of bullying. Some students are taunted and tormented, while others are persecuted by cyber-bullying. Some students are circled on the playground or in other locations in the school away from teachers' notice and physically abused or exposed to relational aggression, in which case they are socially excluded by their classmates and are recipients of negative and sometimes devastating rumors, and friendship withdrawal. Obviously, its purpose is to blatantly damage a classmate's social relationships and acceptance (Simmons, 2002).

Relational aggression is particularly insidious because its victims often allow themselves to be attacked out of a desire to fit in or because they fear further ostracism (Mullin-Rindler, 2003). It is common for groups of girls who are members of a clique to band together and target their victims. The result is loneliness, isolation, depression, and a negative self-concept on the part of victims. Research shows that relational aggression is an outgrowth of clique members' social-psychological maladjustment (Espelage, Mebane, & Swearer, 2004).

Relational aggression in the form of cyber-bullying often takes place away from school. It is carried out with the use of the Internet and other electronic means. Though cyber-bullying is less physical, it nonetheless is devastatingly brutal. Belligerent students use e-mail, cell phones and text messages, instant messaging, defamatory personal websites, and online personal polling websites to support hostility toward their intended victims. This kind of bullying has become very common and is particularly popular among girls, because it can be accomplished without physical confrontation.

In addition, girls can band together in their attacks to increase the potency of their assaults. Because of the nature of the electronic communication technologies, it is possible for bullies to send negative gossip to a large audience without disclosing their true identity. Abusers can simply hide behind an online screen name. Humiliated students find it nearly impossible to escape their tormenters because they can be followed home. In addition, some cell phones have the ability to send text messages, pictures, and even live video. As pointed out earlier, this makes it possible for perverted bullies to spread derogatory information in the form of pictures taken of unsuspecting classmates in compromising places like P.E. locker rooms (Keith & Martin, 2005).

Children ordinarily attempt to acquire love and acceptance through behavior designed to get attention. At a very early age, children seem perpetually involved in trying to get their parents' attention even when this is anticipated to be negative. Negative attention is pursued because of the dearth of positive attention, and because children find it to be a more dependable way to get the attention they desire. They find their positive actions are often ignored by parents who are preoccupied with their own lives. When this routinely occurs, children engage in more upsetting behavior, which more predictably gets their parents' notice.

In addition, children often want more attention than parents and teachers can, or are willing to, provide. When their aspirations are unsatisfied, children customarily resort to more outlandish measures. In the classroom, these efforts are usually disruptive. It is obviously difficult and perhaps impossible to provide all the attention children seek in a class of 30 or more students. However, it must be remembered that students' need for love and acceptance is validated substantially by the attention they get. It seems evident that teachers should try to provide more attention than they routinely do.

More commonly in the complex workings of daily routines in the classroom, it is simpler to shut off the deluge of demands students make for attention though various control techniques. Unfortunately these techniques not only keep students from acquiring desired attention, they often reduce the satisfaction of other associated needs, like the craving for autonomy and control. When these needs go unmet, teachers can expect an increased level of classroom disruptions while thwarted students try to satisfy their needs in increasingly deviant ways. Teachers should take note of the fact that attention needs are much less likely to be fulfilled in classrooms with limited student interaction. Ironically, many teachers erroneously presume that active student participation in class only leads to misbehavior.

It is wise to think of gratifying students' needs as preventive discipline, for that is what it is. When teachers spend more of their time fulfilling student needs, they can anticipate a corresponding reduction in the amount of time necessary to deal with student disruptiveness. Teachers should acknowledge that many of the classroom discipline problems occur simply because students' needs go unfulfilled. The solution is to create strategies for need fulfillment that transcend the usual lack.

This is not a prescriptive endeavor. In other words, teachers cannot be successful with a list of things that will ensure their students obtain what they seek. They must examine the possibilities that are contained within the confines of their curriculum and methods. For example, if instructional strategies include learning communities, the teacher may employ reciprocal care-giving activities as an essential part of group learning. This might consist, for example, of having students look for the positive things done by group members that have significantly contributed to learning.

When children behave disruptively in an effort to satisfy their needs, if teachers react, the result ordinarily is for the aberrant behavior to be reinforced. To avoid this, teachers must help their students satisfy their needs before they find it necessary to engage in aberrant behavior in an effort to gratify themselves. In this way much inappropriate behavior can be avoided.

The need to belong is commonly thwarted in school due to the formation of cliques, as well as to teachers' insensitivity. Though the need for belonging may be spoken of by teachers in various settings, in the classroom other concerns commonly take precedence over fulfilling this need. Thus, even though it may be vaguely recognized as essential, it may not be consistently and coherently provided. Children who feel they don't belong often either act out or become withdrawn. Sometimes depression or suicide are the outcomes. For these children, death is more desirable than living with the pain of loneliness.

Some children's behavior is thought to be abnormal by their peers. These are the youngsters who are customarily ignored or rejected. They are also singled out and tormented. Many times the differences are a function of race and/or class or country of origin and culture. In America this has always been the case in many schools, and in recent years it has become even more so. Teachers need to love and accept all students unconditionally. Students must be taught to do the same.

Children require repeated confirmation that they are accepted for who they are, despite their race and social class or previous low academic achievements and lack of involvement in various extracurricular activities. These characteristics should never be allowed to define them as different in detrimental ways. Rather, the differences between children should be celebrated for the contribution they can make to the lives of all class members. There is a potential for all students to have their lives enriched and to have their understanding of the world greatly enhanced when they truly learn to understand and accept classmates who come from various backgrounds.

Because children's degree of acceptance is validated by unconditional love and understanding, teachers should make sure that all educational events and activities are the epitome of caring and acceptance. They themselves should never be guilty of making remarks that can be interpreted as conditional. Many times statements are made that are not free of the conditions that have unthinkingly been communicated to children with the intention of helping them improve their behavior. For example, a teacher may say, "I'm happy when you make good grades." This statement seems benign enough in terms of detriment. However, it implies that the teacher's happiness is dependent on their students getting good grades. What are children to think of themselves if they get poor grades?

Love is conditional any time acceptance appears to depend on conforming to expectations. Remember, it doesn't matter what the teacher intends, only how students interpret their teachers' statements and actions. For this reason, teachers need to tune in to how students respond to their declarations. Only then can they be assured that conditions for love and acceptance are being properly declared.

Control and Empowerment

School procedures and regulations, as well as teachers' classroom directives, are often unsettling to students. Yet most teachers believe that they must enforce these expectations and always be in control so that students don't get out of hand, become disruptive, and fail to achieve classroom objectives. They are inclined to become so preoccupied with ensuring their own agendas are met that they give very little thought to the fact that their students have just as compelling a need to control their environment. The difference lies mostly in the fact that teachers are generally empowered to enforce school rules whether or not they conflict with the needs of their students. Students are given a much lower priority, and, in most cases, teachers fail to properly recognize students' needs and consequently become obstacles to children satisfying them.

Because they don't recognize children's need for personal control or perhaps are unwilling to accept it, teachers routinely deny children the opportunity to satisfy this need. It is commonly asserted that children are too immature to responsibly regulate their own lives. It is assumed that they will make many mistakes, all to their detriment, and that teachers are only helping prevent the inevitable. Students' need for self-determination is thus dismissed with little thought. However, given sufficient autonomy, students aspire to master particular skills and concepts, and while engaging in high levels of responsible self-regulation, use cognitive strategies that lead to higher levels of achievement as compared to their peers who do not have high autonomy-related mastery aspirations (Pizzolato & Slatton, 2007).

When, because of teachers' desire to be in control, children are denied opportunities to assert themselves and consequently rebel, teachers ordinarily increasingly control them. This only inspires increased student rebellion and an accompanying escalation in teacher control. Disruptiveness can spiral up until teachers are compelled to take drastic measures like recommending students be expelled from school.

It is ironic that students' rebellion is promoted in the beginning by excessive control and that control is the usual means by which teachers and school administrators attempt to quell it. As will repeatedly be mentioned, teachers and administrators attempt to solve discipline problems with their cause. When teachers stimulate rebellion in this way and consequently punish children who act out, they further reinforce bad behavior, which then usually becomes far more difficult to eradicate. Many of these problems can be prevented if teachers recognize that students do indeed have a need to at least be partly in control of what happens to them.

Students' need for control is not just a desire to regulate their school work. They require more control over how their other needs are to be met. Interestingly, each individual has a personal, distinctive way to achieve what they desire and at the same time very little insight regarding the need-fulfilling strategies employed by associates. Because of this, a particular individual may not be very accepting of another's idiosyncratic need-fulfillment schemes. This includes teachers who commonly find it difficult to understand how their students could possibly find satisfaction in some of the ways they behave. They flatly reject certain behaviors as truly need satisfying.

Some of these behaviors, such as fighting, bringing weapons to school, taking drugs, or engaging in premarital sex, may be categorically harmful. Yet even potentially harmful behavior is engaged in by children to in some way satisfy their needs. Despite the fact that certain behaviors may be aberrant and unquestionably injurious, students may see them as the only viable way to satisfy needs that have gone unfulfilled in the normal course of classroom instruction. Interestingly, these aberrations often represent an adjustment made after legitimate, futile attempts to fulfill needs have failed.

Sometimes these antisocial behaviors are just a call for help. At other times, they represent an extreme reaction to excessive control in too many situations for too long a time. It should also be noted that adolescents often find self-regulation regarding unpopular or uncommon goals unacceptable because they typically seek to regulate their behavior such that it fits in with their peer group. Thus, autonomy that is limited to alternatives that students and their peers find aversive as a group is not motivating (Pizzolato & Slatton, 2007).

It should be evident that personal control is a predominant need for everyone, including teachers and their students. This, of course, sets up a potential conflict between over-controlling teachers and the inherent desire their students have for autonomy. But even when teachers have in mind offering their students more autonomy in the classroom, they may not provide it, for research shows that there is a significant difference between the amount of autonomy teachers claim to provide their students and the degree of autonomy students report receiving in the classroom (Edwards & Allred, 1990).

Teachers should not simply renounce students' need for control and personal empowerment. It is a legitimate need. However, children need to be taught how to use personal empowerment in ways that do not thwart its continued use. This means they must learn to satisfy their control need appropriately, not just as a way to dominate and manipulate others or to sabotage the classroom learning atmosphere. This may be difficult for some students, because it is likely that most of the examples they have seen regarding the exercise of power are of the domineering kind. It is unlikely they have experienced power being used in legitimate ways, devoid of subverting the self-determination needs of others. This can be most successfully accomplished when students are taught to only satisfy their needs in conjunction with their efforts to ensure classmates have the same privilege. To do this, they must be helped to understand the necessity of balancing need gratification.

Because each person can experience internal conflicts in satisfying all their needs, and because fulfilling one's needs can conflict with others' efforts to satisfy their needs, a balance must be created. Between-individual balancing is a matter of assuring that all persons in a social group satisfy their needs to the greatest extent possible given the possibility of conflicts. For example, an individual may desire the love and acceptance of others, but try to exercise too much control and consequently experience rejection.

Children should be taught to moderate their needs interactively with others in a way that ensures everyone's needs can be met to an acceptable extent. They must realize that any particular need may not always be one hundred percent satisfied, but that it can be sufficiently fulfilled so that perpetual gratification of all needs is possible. In order to acquire group acceptance, each individual must be willing to forfeit some of his or her desire to control and learn to moderate need satisfaction within a social context.

The Need for Freedom

In balancing their needs, children must learn that it is impossible to achieve all they might desire. They need help in examining all their needs and determining how to balance them appropriately. In particular, the desire for control must always be balanced with the need for love and acceptance. The same is true of control and the need for freedom. Everyone wants sufficient freedom, but their freedom is likely to be constrained if they get rebellious. Essentially people want complete freedom from control by others but to be empowered to control whatever and whomever they wish.

Very young children find it hard understand why this is not possible. If they fail to eventually understand the need to balance control and freedom, they will no doubt experience considerable difficulty successfully interacting with others. They must eventually learn that they cannot completely fulfill all of their needs to the extent they wish. Teachers obviously are involved in students' struggle to acquire an appropriate balance between freedom and control. As already mentioned, teachers not only have to deal with their personal desire to control, but also with how their role as a teacher gets defined by themselves and others because of assumed student immaturity.

Faced with excessive control in the classroom, students often wish for more freedom. Unfortunately, it is difficult for both students and teachers to properly calculate the appropriate amount of freedom that should be offered. This is not only because of preexisting ideas about freedom and control, but also because of the various degree of readiness of students to responsibly use their autonomy. Often the very students who make the most strident demands for more freedom are the ones least capable of using their autonomy responsibly. Such behavior invariably leads teachers to deny greater freedom to all students.

Along with this, teachers are unlikely to help students learn to moderate need satisfaction as described above. For many teachers the potential for student readiness for self-government goes unnoticed, while for others it is too burdensome. It is much easier to unequivocally deny students the opportunity for growth in balancing their needs within a social context. By failing to recognize the need students have for learning to moderate their needs, teachers' failure is guaranteed. It certainly won't occur to students that need balancing is essential.

Instead of empowering students through an increasing degree of autonomy, many teachers handicap their students with reduced freedom and excessive control as time goes by. More rebellion is the obvious student reaction. Teachers accept this as a confirmation of students' inherent irresponsibility. Even when children simply get out of hand in an over-exuberant effort to have fun, teachers often react negatively and conclude that the children are unable to use freedom wisely. It would be unusual for teachers to conclude that they themselves are the primary instigators of student unruliness when they do not consistently help students learn to properly balance their needs.

The need for autonomy is inherent in all human beings. It is asserted by children long before they are capable of acting upon it responsibly. Even when conscientious teachers try to help students recognize the gradual emergence of their capability to be self-governing, and try to teach them how to prepare themselves, students typically wish to exceed the reasonable limits placed upon them. However, the usual scenario is for teachers to consider students' efforts to acquire more freedom as affronts to their authority.

In addition, they routinely doubt the ability of students to use their freedom responsibly. Thus, opportunities for free expression or even learning about how to express themselves responsibly is withheld pending evidence of maturity. But freedom is a necessary component of learning how to be responsible. It therefore cannot be employed as a reward for becoming more trustworthy. The appropriate strategy is for teachers to provide an increasing level of freedom as students show an inclination and ability to use it wisely.

The nature of this gradual increase should be taught to students interactively so that they are involved in achieving an understanding of the appropriate degree of agency they can obtain given their level of maturity. They should also learn that their teacher's purpose is to fully empower them. Along with this, they must realize that their excessive desire for autonomy may keep them from achieving it as quickly as they hope. In the process they should learn to appreciate that balancing their needs with those of others in society is essential, and that failure to do so will likely produce more restrictions, not less.

In an effort to help their students raise the level of responsibility and associated autonomy, teachers should help them develop decision-making skills. Even young children can learn to make valid decisions about many issues that concern them and to discover how to meet the problems they will inevitably encounter in the future. Their decision-making opportunities need to go beyond class rules or topics to be studied and include critical decisions about all aspects of a properly functioning learning community. This involves determinations about the learning process, the functioning of the learning community, processes that promote an atmosphere of care, how evaluation should take place, how to negotiate conflicts over various group matters, discipline issues, and so forth.

Students also need to consider what the future may bring and how to best prepare for it. One cannot assume all things will remain the same. Though students can't always validly predict everything that will happen in the future, they must learn how to anticipate much of what might take place as they explore various historical perspectives as well as predictions about changes in the physical world, their future employment prospects, the implications associated with various social happenings, what might happen in the case of various catastrophic events, and the like. They need to learn decision making within school, family, society, employment, and other possible contexts. These should include historical implications, current reality, and future possibilities.

In making various determinations, children should recognize potential consequences of these decisions. Deciding on a course of action should not simply be a matter of selecting among options provided by the teacher. Students need to formulate the possibilities themselves. Each prospect should be accompanied by associated likely consequences. Students need to experience the process of assessing alternatives and consequences and deciding on the best approach to various problems and tasks.

Children are usually unfamiliar with the nature of responsibility as they examine potential consequences. They may not fully realize the consequences they can expect from specific choices they make. Many times parents and teachers shield students from experiencing the consequences of their actions. These consequences include natural ones as well as those contrived by parents and teachers. Eventually children must learn that freedom validly exists only when they regulate their own behavior while carefully taking consequences into account. Ignoring consequences may deprive them of the freedom they fervently seek. For example, children who fail to take the consequences of illicit drug use into account will undoubtedly find themselves hooked and perhaps overdosed or incarcerated.

Self-Mastery and Competence

Intellectual competence is usually considered to be the primary goal of schooling, and helping children achieve a sense of competency satisfies a very important need. Competence is, in part, obtained by students demonstrating various skills that others value (Coopersmith, 1967). But it is also important that they satisfy themselves regarding their competency in a number of areas. This should not consist exclusively of passing tests and demonstrating achievement on various teacher evaluations. Nor should competence expectations be modified in order to make students feel good about their school performances. When this is done, students often recognize the disparity between their real accomplishments and those teachers falsify to bolster their self-concepts.

When students see through this deception, they are left with the realization that they have accomplished significantly less than they have been led to believe because of being beguiled by their teachers. Unfortunately, to be singled out for deceptive help communicates to students that they are considered incompetent. Students need to appreciate their true capabilities, not inflated ones. This gives them a better picture of what they must do to accomplish what they wish. They also should not be deceived about their possibilities.

Students also should not be led to believe they can do things of which they are incapable. For example, a student who is 5 feet 4 inches tall is unlikely to succeed as a professional basketball player. In addition, children should not be undersold regarding their capabilities. They should be helped to have a realistic perception of their current level of expertise along with a valid picture of what it will take to achieve what they desire. In doing this, students should not have to rely exclusively on the assessments of their teachers. Teachers won't always be on hand to make these judgments. Instead children should learn to assess their own capabilities and competencies. It is critical to realize that teachers who falsely elevate the accomplishments of their students run the risk of promoting poor self-concept and depression to go along with low achievement (Seligman, 1995).

In cultivating student competence, schools ordinarily do not provide students many opportunities to think about problems and create problem-solving strategies. In fact, many students are thought to be incapable of logical thinking. However, even children can think logically. In thinking, conclusions may be reached that other people dispute, not because logic was not exercised, but because there are different points of view (Smith, 1990).

To make the learning environment consistent with the way children think, teachers must provide their students the opportunity to frame their own questions and then help them engage in inquiry research. The research questions should be personally meaningful and relevant. In carrying out their research, students should be encouraged to monitor their own thinking, carefully checking for unsupported assumptions and various kinds of inconsistencies.

Once students obtain results from their research, they should be encouraged to present their findings to other class members. In this process they should compare their conclusions with the opinions of their peers. Viable alternative points of view should be identified in addition to searching for hidden assumptions and alternative explanations. In a thinking classroom, students are encouraged to dissect, reflect on, and modify what they find in their research, including what they read, hear, see, or feel, and increase the complexity of their understanding by interacting with their peers.

Decision making requires not only basic intellectual skills, but also necessary associated information. This is an area that allows students to determine their intellectual competence for themselves. This can be done by comparing decisions made with results obtained. When decisions result in proper consequences, students are able to credit themselves with an appropriate level of competency. When bad decisions are made, students should accept them as part of the learning experience rather than as outcomes that are catastrophically final. New decisions can be made that take into account what students learn from their mistakes.

Competence also involves a genuine understanding of one's self as well as others. Psychological and social capabilities are both part of the critical knowledge students should obtain in their school experiences. Full participation in a learning community that employs democratic principles is perhaps the best environment for social and psychological competence. The dynamics of social discourse can best be learned and appreciated within a context of complex interactions, which are routinely provided in learning communities.

In this environment, children can learn strategies for successfully interacting with others. They can discover how to create an environment of care and exercise appropriate leadership during the course of complicated interactions with others. Because one's own psychological well-being depends on successful social relationships, students are able to obtain a more complete understanding of their own psychological life and direct it in positive ways.

Social interactions should always include a sense of moral responsibility. Under the right instructional conditions, social connections between students can provide a context in which moral judgment and accountability are encouraged. It is essential that teachers understand the levels of moral reasoning so that they can help encourage the kind of social interactions and discussions that dependably aid students to become more sophisticated moral reasoners.

Lawrence Kohlberg (1969, 1973, 1976) provides descriptions of growth stages for moral reasoning that define the kind of thinking and actions that are indicators of a particular level of development. His research indicates that one's competence for moral reasoning can be accentuated to some degree by confronting moral dilemmas. This proficiency is a particularly potent need, as students interact with their peers and others in their quest to become more accepted and socially influential.

As children's intellectual ability advances, they become more able to function at higher moral reasoning levels. Initially they reason in response to potential punishment. After this they think in terms of what must be done to acquire approval. The next stage is a legalistic one in which the individual acts upon the expectations of the greater community. Finally, the individual's moral thinking becomes congruent with universal principles and their actions consistent with human dignity.

Social Needs

Social needs are inextricably connected with personal desires. It isn't always easy to see how to satisfy both personal and social demands. The issue for children is to regulate personal behavior so as not to alienate others and jeopardize their chances of social fulfillment while at the same time satisfying personal aspirations to the greatest extent possible. In the beginning, young children rarely think about satisfying the needs of others. Thus, even when they are taught the necessity of sharing, they may temporarily forgo seeking what they want, but eventually they will simply ignore what others expressly want and pursue their own agenda with little or no regard for associates.

Under the proper learning conditions they eventually discover that their needs cannot be exclusively sought. Any time they only pursue their own agenda, they find out that most of their needs go unmet because associates are reluctant to tolerate their actions when they don't show them due consideration. And without meaningful interactions, it is impossible to have authentic need-satisfying experiences.

As mentioned previously, children must eventually learn their needs can only be adequately met within a social context. That is because almost all human needs are socially oriented. For example, control can only be exercised within social interactions and activities, as is also true of the need for fun. Love and acceptance must be provided by associates. Freedom is usually exercised in connection with social relationships. In the schools, this is best supported by an instructional program that focuses on community-oriented learning opportunities.

Perhaps the most satisfying social experiences involve actions that make a difference in someone else's life. This, of course, requires students to be as much concerned for others as they are for themselves. The best way to promote this attitude is to encourage children to serve each other. In a learning community this may include helping a classmate understand difficult concepts or aiding him or her in completing a project. Students might also help protect classmates from being bullied. Students can become more fully satisfied in a social sense when they are significantly involved in helping others succeed academically, and genuinely revel in their success.

The Need for Fun

Glasser (1984, 1998) believes that one of our basic needs is having fun. Children's need for fun is evident in their ordinary query to each other as they discuss various activities, "Was it fun?" When they are not enjoying themselves, they often declare they are bored. Young children appear to have an unending quest to have fun. In most of their play, that's what they have in mind. Sometimes fun means winning in various contests they concoct in their play. Other times just participating suffices. Children who need to be victorious in all their play activities usually alienate playmates and consequently forfeit the social structure that would have helped them satisfy their need for fun. Ordinarily they fail to see that they have a responsibility to help playmates have fun in order to court their favor.

Children are driven by the need for fun to a greater extent than parents and teachers are usually willing to accommodate. They are apparently afraid that children will be "spoiled" if they play too much, so a requisite amount of work is ordinarily assigned to keep things in balance. This usually leaves children unsatisfied, so they rebel. Teachers also commonly believe in the false admonition that learning is not fun. Instead they see it as work that must be done and sacrifices that must be made. Thus, they contrive all sorts of inducements to get children to do what they realize is unpleasant to them.

Prior to entering school children willingly and enthusiastically learn all day long. It is a significant part of their play. Once enrolled in school, however, learning becomes the kind of effort many prefer to avoid. Some children become willing conscripts because they are routinely rewarded for their achievements. Rewards eventually become more enticing to them than learning itself. Thus, what was formerly learned because it was intrinsically interesting eventually must be encouraged through a reward–punishment system. What could have perpetuated continued interest in learning is the inherent question. Ensuring that learning is genuinely fun is at least part of the answer.

The learning children are involved in before school is obviously fun to them, partly from sheer enjoyment, partly from satisfying their curiosity about the world in which they live, and partly from using what they learn to skillfully manipulate things as they wish and perhaps achieve a sense of competence. They seem compelled to understand what is going on around them in an effort to more readily know what is happening and be able to react appropriately.

At this time most of their learning efforts are self-directed. Herein may be the reason school learning is unappealing. Natural learning has a self-directed orientation and is spurred on by personal curiosity about what is observed during daily activities. At home they are not ordinarily forced to pursue learning. Thus, their personal interests form the basis for their daily investigations. They are also not directed to learn in a set way for a given period of time in close coordination with a classroom of peers.

The closer schools can come to promoting learning as it is naturally engaged in by children, the more students will be encouraged to learn effectively. Learning should thus be more fun because it is more personally meaningful. This doesn't mean that each child should pursue learning in the absence of peers. In their play, children need to be meaningfully associated with age-mates. Children's learning can, therefore, be made more motivating, meaningful, and fun when it involves classmates and when children have genuine opportunities to direct their own learning. Learning communities provide a proper format for this kind of learning.

Learning may also be judged as fun by students when it helps them accomplish various tasks in which they have an interest. They can be genuinely turned on by learning that allows them to be more responsibly self-directed and able to meaningfully pursue their various interests. For example, learning to tie flies for fishing may seem to be a topic that is completely out of bounds in a biology course. However, students may be motivated to learn more in depth about insects and other animals that fish commonly pursue if it is connected to something they find enjoyable, like fishing. This is particularly so when the task is challenging and when considerable depth of understanding is needed. Further motivation can be achieved when students are encouraged to engage in their own research to find out answers to their questions about the insects and their life-cycles. They might even engage in research projects about fish. Perhaps some will even become motivated to learn about insects as disease vectors. This could open up their interests to a broad range of important biological topics.

Being self-directed is far more fun than having someone else tell you what to do. Many of the topics routinely taught in school would be more enjoyable if they incorporated more opportunities for students to help direct their own learning. Often students withdraw from engagement in what they might otherwise find significant and rewarding simply because of being forced to learn in a particular way and according to a predetermined time schedule. By definition this takes away the fun. It is important to realize that there are variations in what children find enjoyable in school. Sometimes they just need the latitude of studying a particular topic in an unusual way. Other times they need an entirely different topic than their classmates.

The need for enjoyment is not confined to children and youth. Even adults have a greater need for fun than they ordinarily admit. One has only to consider the multibillion-dollar industries that supply adults with ever-increasing opportunities and materials to satisfy their need for "fun." Unfortunately, adults in their quest to make sure children learn to work and study hard forget that fun is a basic human need. They typically misapply the term *fun* exclusively to forms of entertainment.

Many meaningful experiences that are assumed to simply be work can provide fun and enjoyment along with a real sense of satisfaction so long as they are not structured in ways that eliminate fun. In the adult world, individuals seem compelled to pursue many meaningful activities that some would call work, but which they consider inherently pleasurable. They pursue them because they bring a sense of accomplishment, which in the final analysis is simply fun.

The Need for Fantasy

Though not often thought of as an inherent need, fantasy plays an enormous role in the lives of children and is the antecedent to many accomplishments in the adult world as well. Teachers usually look upon fantasy as a waste of time. Often it is considered a threat to their authority as children "daydream" instead of doing assigned work. However, fantasizing is a vitalizing activity, and to force children to abandon their natural inclination to fantasize is more harmful than helpful.

Fantasy fuels creativity. It is the source of inspiration by which artists paint, musicians compose, and poets write. It is also the genesis of scientific research, governmental problem solving, and a host of other important human activities. All humans need creativity in their lives to achieve their full potential. Permitting children the option of engaging in activities that grow out of their fantasies empowers them to deal more effectively with life's complexities and problems, satisfies a very basic need, and promotes a sense of well-being. It would be well in fact for teachers to set aside a time for fantasy as well as opportunities for students to bring their fantasies to fruition.

Perhaps the greatest obstacle teachers face in promoting such learning is the pressure they feel to cover "the curriculum" so that students are able to pass examinations. Teachers might well ask whether it is more important for students to memorize such things as the structure of plants and the orders of insects or conduct a successful science project in which they come up with interesting ideas and questions and effectively engage in appropriately designed research to answer their questions. Teachers must consider the fact that fantasy is a natural, healthy pursuit in which all children engage, and that it can lead to many worthwhile learning experiences. Teachers must also abandon the inclination to look at children's daydreaming as a threat to proper school activities.

There is no doubt that some children daydream in response to learning activities they find meaningless and boring. Intelligent teachers use such cues to evaluate their teaching. Fantasy may also be used by students as an escape from conditions in school that make them feel unaccepted or threatened. Here again fantasizing is not a menace to children, but only a threat to the teacher's desire for students' undivided attention.

Students' fantasies can be responsibly directed by teachers who engage in fantasy-based creative activities themselves. This not only helps students learn to empower their fantasizing inclinations, but also discover that such behavior is not only legitimate, but also growth enhancing.

TRENDS RELATED TO NEED FULFILLMENT

It has become more popular to address student needs in discussions about schooling. It is particularly so among educational theorists who focus upon topics such as contrasts between the nature of learning and school practices (Darling-Hammond, 1997; Kohn, 1998), the causes of bullying and violence in the schools (Coleman, 2002; Espelage, Mebane, & Swearer, 2004; Smith, 2004), discipline problems (Glasser, 1998, 2005; Kohn, 1996, 1998; Brophy, 2004; Butchart, 1998), caring relationships (Noddings, 1992, 1993, 2002), learning communities (Watkins, 2005; Sergiovanni, 1990, 1994), and child and youth depression (Seligman, 1995). Need fulfillment is seen as a critical aspect of schools that has enormous implications for academic achievement as well as appropriate social and psychological development. It is clear that unfulfilled needs are behind many common school problems (Glasser, 1998).

Currently there is a move to modify school standards and accompanying practices to be consistent with the needs of both students and modern society. This has come in the form of student empowerment, democratic discipline, student self-direction, academic competence, an ethic of care, and learning communities.

Chapter Three

Democratic Discipline and Student Empowerment

The object of democratic discipline is not just to maintain order in the classroom and other areas of the school. Rather it is a comprehensive plan that is inextricably interwoven with all aspects of schooling, particularly the curriculum and instruction program. In providing a proper context for effective learning, discipline procedures must accommodate individual student differences while catering to their need for meaningful interaction with peers. In addition, discipline should promote students' self-concept and achievement and help provide an avenue for students to become fully integrated into the school society as well as society at large.

It is critical that discipline procedures accentuate the social and psychological well-being of students and help them to fully satisfy their needs. As discussed earlier, discipline should never be divorced from learning as if they are two different processes requiring different sets of principles for implementation. The same principles should apply to both. The most effective discipline is simply an integrated extension of the instructional program.

Choosing to discipline democratically is based not only on the potential for incurring fewer problems, but also because it fits inherently within democratic communities and is consistent with basic human functioning. The quest for personal freedom is a central feature of nearly all human endeavors (Glasser, 1998). It appears early in the lives of children as evidenced by their striving for independence as they learn and experience the world. Even as toddlers they often insist on accomplishing tasks like tying their shoes or running the vacuum cleaner long before they are able to successfully do these things by themselves.

The desire for freedom is always with us, and much of human thought and energy is devoted to acquiring and maintaining agency despite the restrictive efforts of others. This is particularly evident in schools where the autonomy of children is routinely limited in order to carry out the program of instruction in designated ways.

When children's freedom is challenged, they predictably rebel. This is particularly so during adolescence when young people are attempting to attain adult status. They see themselves as capable of doing many things that were earlier denied them because of their size or lack of maturity. As they emerge into adulthood, youth often react to efforts to restrict them, while adults constrain them until they are satisfied the youth have the proper education, skills, and sense of responsibility needed to function in the adult world. These restrictions are not unilaterally needed, because many youth already possess the skills and attitudes required to successfully function as adults. However their readiness is sometimes discredited by aberrant behavior brought on by being excessively restricted.

Predictably, adults choose to see youth as immature when they react to control tactics. So an impasse is born of children's conviction that they can act responsibly and adults' lack of confidence in them. Children inherently want more freedom, but adults are fearful of their supposed lack of judgment and the potentially devastating consequences of decisions they may make. Many times the outlandish behavior of a few youth is used to label and restrict them all as a group. The necessity for educating youth for responsible decision making is ordinarily not considered, as if maturity were a matter of age rather than education and experience.

The willingness of some children to follow their teachers' directions may not come from their confidence in the judgment and experience of their mentors. Rather, it may be because they see no alternative but to submit to adult directions. That is because adults are the gatekeepers to rewards and attractive vocations. Without adult help and supervision young people would be left without the necessary resources to achieve their goals. Because adults hold the keys to the future for youth, many willingly submit to unnecessary control. For their part, teachers believe they act appropriately when they control excessively, ostensibly to protect the school learning environment from anticipated student unruliness. Their assumptions likely have been repeatedly but spuriously "confirmed" by children's imprudent reactions to adult coercion.

Ironically, adults are unlikely to believe their coercive strategies are the cause of student rebellion. Rather, they simply attribute misbehavior to the inherent nature of youth or their home environment. Unfortunately, when children are denied their freedom in the process of achieving greater personal responsibility, they are missing the most critical ingredient in this process. Children can't learn to act responsibly unless they have sufficient freedom. Adults insist that responsibility development must precede the allocation of freedom. Thus, they deny youth the most necessary constituent for learning to be responsible and in the process promote the very problems they are trying to eliminate.

It may be difficult for teachers to visualize how student autonomy can be an integral part of children's school experiences. Instead they may believe such a learning configuration requires firm control to avoid potential disruptions. However, student autonomy is an essential part of successful school learning and it in turn provides valid preparation for life outside of school. Thus, autonomy is not only an essential ingredient for independence, it is an essential component of democratic communities. As mentioned earlier, this is because most individuals desire sufficient autonomy along with community membership.

Satisfying human needs requires interactions with others. That includes sufficient autonomy within the community to satisfy the need for personal freedom. Thankfully community affairs can include sufficient freedom for all members to satisfy their need for autonomy without subverting the cooperation necessary to achieve their socially related requirements. When personal autonomy is excessively restricted in community interactions, community life stagnates and many personal needs go unfulfilled.

In order to maintain an atmosphere of freedom in learning communities, each member must be encouraged to make many self-generated contributions that the individual believes are helpful to the group. To do this, they must be personally motivated and their contributions allowed to evolve from personal interests and desires rather than teacher assignments. This way personal commitment is promoted and the quality of each member's work encouraged. In this configuration, each individual's contribution can be unique and based on personal interests and qualifications.

Each student has the responsibility to determine how he or she might best serve the learning community while at the same time satisfying personal needs. School learning should be routinely related to students' everyday experiences in order to infuse motivation with personal interest. Also students must be provided ways to make sense of current experiences relative to the past, and enabled to make valid, insightful decisions regarding matters they consider important (Glickman, 1993; Meier, 2002; Starratt, 1996).

STUDENT EMPOWERMENT

To become self-disciplined, learners must become empowered by authentic membership in learning communities. As bonafide members, students experience the resolute respect of their peers, which evolves out of having true regard for one another as unique individuals. Because communities are made up of a variety of participants with various differences, it is necessary that these idiosyncracies be celebrated and learned from rather than discriminated against.

Respect requires not only genuine courtesy; there must also be an unquestionable sense of care. Members must reach out to each other, routinely initiate positive interactions, and engage in actions that not only increase acceptance, but also loyalty and understanding. This comes about by sharing a common culture and values in which conduct and expectations are universally accepted. Thus, students focus their attention on unity rather than being pitted against each other, as is often the case in traditional schools. This is essential to discipline in democratic learning communities.

Children are empowered in authentic learning communities because they know they are genuinely accepted, carefully listened to, and taken seriously. They know they not only will be protected from intentional hurt, but can expect classmates to come to their aid if they are attacked elsewhere by bullies. Empowerment also includes the opportunity to have authentic decision-making power, which is not routinely scrutinized for potential veto by their teachers. Instead they are secure in knowing they are engaged in a process of increasingly acquiring group and individual decision-making rights, which are screened primarily by other members of the group.

Leadership increasingly comes from the group. Teachers relinquish leadership responsibilities as students gradually become more able to provide it. In this process, students are able to better discern their relative growth in responsible decision making because their contributions are respected despite their age and inexperience. As individual and group decisions are made, students' interests are accepted as valid and are appreciated as an integral part of the group learning process. Individuals so empowered have little inclination to disrupt the ongoing affairs of the group.

When students feel the sincere regard of their classmates while acquiring a sense of empowerment, strong interpersonal attachments evolve and group commitment develops. Commitment energizes students to vigorously engage in the work of the learning community. In the process, a sense of family is produced where there are shared goals and values. Individuals in a learning community only become empowered when the schools see fit to decentralize operations and reduce the bureaucratic functions that stand in the way of truly empowering students and their teachers in individual classrooms (Hiatt & Diana, 2001). This includes matters of discipline as well as the instructional program.

In describing student empowerment in a democratic learning community, it is critical to differentiate between legal and moral democracy. In most cases, the laws that are employed to govern a group of people are enacted by representatives. To encourage members to abide by the laws, punishments are imposed on violators.

In a moral democracy, students are empowered to act as they see fit, so long as they don't impose on the liberties and well-being of classmates. In this case, punishments are not prescribed for violating laws. Instead discussions are held in an effort to clarify matters relating to various problems and commitments are made to allow moral principles to govern behavior. Students avoid disrupting class, not because they fear applicable punishments, but because, in the interest of both themselves and their classmates, they prefer to protect the learning environment. Thus, student actions are governed by conscience rather than imposed rules and fear of retribution (Kohlberg, 1969, 1976).

STUDENTS' REACTIONS TO SCHOOL-BASED AUTHORITY

The growth of student responsibility and empowerment always includes a requisite amount of freedom. How much freedom is provided is governed by the strategies and purposes of the empowerment efforts of teachers. Thus, a child doesn't earn the right to freedom by behaving as directed. Instead, student autonomy is an integral part of the process of teaching children to be responsibly free. Students don't have to first prove their ability to be self-governing before being allowed self-determination. Rather they are viewed as being in the process of discovering how to responsibly manage themselves by being extended sufficient freedom to make important decisions about their own learning, as well as appropriate classroom operations.

Classrooms do need proper order to promote optimum learning. But the proper learning environment cannot simply be established by carefully regulating all student behavior. More often than not classroom misbehavior can be traced to dysfunctions in the interpersonal climate and organizational pattern of the school than to student causes (Darling-Hammond, 1997). For optimum learning with limited disruptions, students require an accepting, caring environment, one in which they have considerable control over what happens to them as well as opportunities to achieve a true sense of competence.

Personal control is a particularly potent need because it constitutes the impetus through which all other needs are fulfilled. In addition, each individual has a personal view of his or her needs and how best to satisfy them (Glasser, 1984). Even though students may appear to be satisfying their needs in questionable ways, teachers must realize that they believe their efforts are the most satisfying choice available at that particular time. These conceptions make sense to them; otherwise they wouldn't have them (Glasser, 1997a). Consequently, it is very difficult to change their perception of the need gratification process (Glasser, 1997b).

Children do not picture themselves doing badly. Instead they believe their behavior will lead to success and happiness. Even when they behave destructively, they do not intend to hurt themselves, though their teachers may be unable to understand why they don't see their behavior as calamitous. For example, children may believe that taking illicit drugs cannot harm them. The sure pleasure and escape from pain they experience with drugs is hard to abandon and replace with the unpredictable pleasures that can be found in good relationships, achieving competence, and the like.

Power is exercised over students in a number of ways, all of which they are likely to abhor and rebel against. For example, children may have power wielded over them (1) in unexpected ways without warning, (2) for others' personal gain, (3) in an attempt to modify or cancel agreements made earlier, (4) to prove who is the boss, (5) in ignorance of the situation, (6) because it is assumed they are too immature to make their own decisions, (7) to escape responsibility, (8) to impose unnecessary or illogical rules and procedures, (9) when there is a disagreement regarding curriculum and instruction, and (10) to limit student options.

Unfortunately, when there is inappropriate use of power, students may feel unable to make their grievances known with any hope that appropriate actions will be taken to correct them. They may believe that their only recourse is to make life miserable for those in authority (Glasser, 1998). Their negative view of the way authority is implemented in the schools may be generalized to all authority figures (Glasser, 1984). Youth can be expected to react adversely to the abuse of power. It is really no different in the adult population. In contrast, if students are empowered to acquire genuine competency, engage in meaningful interactions with their peers, and help to regulate the instructional program, they will come to understand the appropriate use of power and become more qualified themselves for leadership responsibilities.

AUTONOMY AND LEARNING

Student unruliness is due in large measure to their previous history of being dominated. Students who have previously been governed by the usual school rules and restraints, and then given more freedom, are unlikely to suddenly use their newfound freedom responsibly. Instead they are liable to continue to react negatively, because in the past short episodes of freedom may have been experienced along with the predictable return to authoritarian control as soon as students make rowdy reactions. From their perspective the offer of autonomy may be seen simply as a sign of teacher weakness, a game that is being played, or momentary failure to enforce the teachers' authoritarian role and as an inducement to misbehave.

In response, teachers predictably assume that students are not ready for an increase in freedom and attribute this to inherent disruptiveness. Many times the punitiveness of the teachers' reactions exceeds previous levels, contributing to an increase in student misbehavior. Teachers are unlikely to realize that their own behavior is the major contributor to classroom discipline problems.

One of the reasons that a return to disruptiveness is inevitable once freedom is provided is that other aspects of learning and instruction may remain the same. It is hard to convince students that anything has changed when the instructional program is still primarily teacher directed. Even when the nature of the instructional program is substantially changed, it takes some time before students respond appropriately. Their negative response patterns have usually been a long time in the making. Essentially they have to be deprogrammed over a lengthy period of time.

Students cannot be expected to automatically become more responsible in class simply by receiving more freedom and by teachers declaring their trust. Becoming responsible is not a matter of students' age or teacher edict. Rather, the amount of freedom offered students must be consistent with the level of personal and social responsibility they have already achieved, but with an attached idea of increasing freedom appropriately. When the degree of freedom received by students is consistent with their current level of maturity, and increased as befitting their growth, they are able to gradually achieve a higher level of social responsibility.

It should be reemphasized that responsible autonomy cannot be acquired in the absence of freedom. A proper balance must be struck between developing responsibility and receiving a requisite amount of freedom. This is best accomplished within a classroom format designed to help students focus on real-life problems within a learning community context. Learning communities allow teachers to spend less time monitoring and correcting misbehavior because students are involved in doing this themselves. Teachers are thus able to devote more of their attention to the instructional process. In addition, because students are more self-regulating, they are less inclined to rebel. This approach provides more meaningful experiences for students and helps them learn that many of life's activities have community connections (Sergiovanni, 2000).

Maturity gradually occurs and must be based upon experiences that promote it. The experiences children commonly have in school are not specifically designed for this purpose. It appears that responsibility is expected to occur spontaneously or not at all. Yet the kind of instructional programs most children experience require more and not less teacher control the longer they are in school. Ironically, research shows that elementary school children are allowed to make more decisions regarding their classroom experiences than high school seniors (Goodlad, 1984).

Teachers must be aware of the process children go through as they mature. It should be clear that it requires the development of community relationships and experiences. Jelinek (1979) identifies the following attributes that appear during the process of maturity: (1) Students increasingly become more willing to accept a responsible share of the common human enterprise and gradually become aware that valid, useful experiences are shared. (2) Students become increasingly adept at incorporating natural consequences into their behavior. Natural consequences are thus used to guide their interactions with others and make adjustments to life's problems. (3) Students become increasingly more able to articulate beliefs and opinions and more persuasive in presenting arguments which support their views. (4) Students become more empathetic. They learn to truly appreciate the views of others and become interested in them. (5) Students become more comprehensive and philosophical in developing meanings. In group activities they become more cohesive and productive and become more meaningfully occupied in community affairs and more deeply involved in what others consider significant.

As community affairs become a reflection of the students' important beliefs, their commitment to group learning evolves. Commitment is what drives communities toward more active and fulfilling participation (Sergiovanni, 1992).

Responsible learning must incorporate personal and social values. These are needed in order for members of a learning community to work together successfully. As outlined in Chapter 1, shared values are needed before the entire community can become deeply involved. It is not only necessary for community members to value things in common, they must also know why they value them. This provides for interactions that help to clarify and solidify commitments. It also provides a format within which the need for personal freedom can be related to community action (Sergiovanni, 1994). For example, students might examine their views regarding the homeless in their community and discuss what actions they might take to be involved and helpful. As part of this, they might explore their feelings about the welfare system and the extent to which its operation may be part of the problem. They no doubt would discuss how they feel about those who have the ability to work and choose not to, living instead off the dole. This could be contrasted with those who are temporarily out of work due to situations beyond their control. Research might be done regarding the results of government efforts to help the homeless. Students might, for example, be interested in discovering the extent to which children continue the practice of receiving government assistance like their parents.

The acquisition of meaningful knowledge is central to students becoming more responsibly autonomous. Actually the personally managed search for meaning is a growing experience in and of itself. This quest is accentuated when it is carried out within the social context of a learning community. However, when students do not have a significant role in determining what they learn, and they judge what is expected to be irrelevant, little growth is possible (Darling-Hammond, 1997).

If education proceeds as it should, students can feel empowered by what they learn, particularly when they perceive the knowledge or skills they acquire to be instrumental in achieving their needs and goals (Glasser, 1998). It is unlikely that children will routinely accept learning goals as their own in the absence of self-determination. Without personal involvement they be-grudgingly pursue what they are assigned to learn. More importantly they fail to achieve a sense of empowerment, which could have successfully driven their learning.

AUTONOMY AND ACHIEVEMENT

There is a common assumption that student-directed learning results in low achievement. In reality, when students are allowed to regulate their own learning, they tend to have better achievement results. This is true at various levels in secondary school (Williams, 1996), as well as in the university (Linder & Harris, 1993). Similar results were obtained in research regarding gifted students (DelBello, 1988), children with learning disabilities (Rooney & Hallahan, 1988), and corrections education students (Linder, 1994).

DelBello (1988) discovered that moderately gifted students outdistanced highly gifted peers when their parents had high expectations for them, en-couraged a "can do" attitude, created a balance between structure and free-dom, provided opportunities for children to present their ideas, questioned children rather than controlling their behavior, and encouraged children to make lists, sketch diagrams of proposed projects, and follow self-imposed deadlines. Consequently, with some instruction on decision making along with positive encouragement and an atmosphere of freedom, children can learn to aptly regulate their own learning and achieve at higher levels than more capable but highly controlled peers.

One way government officials and educators manage students is through high-stakes tests. The purpose of these tests is to force greater adherence to national standards. However, some experts see these tests as a threat to standards (Merrow, 2001). It is now evident that imposing high-stakes tests has produced extensive "teaching to the test," in addition to greatly undermining curriculum quality and discriminating against various groups of students (Clinchy, 2001; McNeil, 2000; Nichols & Berliner, 2007).

Ironically, some teachers are required to teach subjects that are covered on the test rather that the content of the courses for which they have been trained. Many times the arts and subjects other than math and English are limited or eliminated from school curricula. In addition, there are some cases where teachers and school administrators have blatantly cheated in an effort to increase student scores. This has been especially so when retaining one's job is contingent on the results (Merrow, 2001; Nichols & Berliner, 2007; Madaus, Russell, & Higgins, 2009).

It is essential that the merits of high-stakes testing be compared with deficits in order to determine if this management tactic really does have worth. Their purpose is solely to use student test scores to force a reframing of education. High-stakes tests place unacceptable restrictions both on teaching and learning. First, they reduce the breadth and fullness of the curriculum and force a narrowing of topics and depth. Second, the mandates that accompany high-stakes testing limit opportunities for students to help make decisions about what and how they learn, thus negating student empowerment. Third, the test-taking scenario conditions students to carefully follow instructions rather than to pursue learning through investigation and inquiry. Fourth, students tend to simply meet standards rather than pursuing excellence. Fifth, there is little assurance that preparing for standardized tests helps students genuinely prepare for life's challenges and expectations. Sixth, high-stakes tests cover such a narrow range of information that they discourage the learning of much of what should justifiably be included in the curriculum as well as skills that are critical to life in a democratic society. Seventh, they fail to focus on the abilities and interests of students.

Fraud and cheating in high-stakes testing is pervasive and instrumental in promoting negative outcomes. Of course many of the instances of cheating go undetected. Unfortunately, when teachers get involved, their position as moral leaders is compromised, due to the untenable position they are put in to ensure their students pass the tests.

Administrators get involved as well by such practices as encouraging low-ability students to drop out of school. Sometimes struggling students are warehoused in the school auditorium during the tests, where they idly sit filling out worksheets. They are not counted among test takers, but fail and eventually drop out of school when they are denied graduation (Nichols & Berliner, 2007).

Students are required by their teachers to spend an inordinate amount of time preparing for high-stakes tests even though they would be better served by using the available time becoming involved in critical learning opportunities (Meier, 2002). Many very valuable learning opportunities are avoided in favor of activities that can be readily measured with multiple-choice test items. This, of course, is the preferred testing format for high-stakes testing. In the process, children lose opportunities to learn what is truly valuable. As a result they miss out on the development of problem-solving and decision-making skills. These are empowering skills not only in adult life, but also to help children deal with current problems and life situations.

Many of the problems children face require greater problem-solving skills than they currently can employ. Their lives are replete with failed decision making that they might have avoided had their schooling prepared them properly. Examples include involvement in gang activity, drug use, sexual promiscuity, and failure to properly focus on their school work.

Few children anticipate problems in order to avoid them or plan how to solve them. They rarely examine the assumptions upon which their decisions are made and similarly fail to use appropriate criteria in judging the appropriateness of their choices. Many children are not working to accomplish long-range goals. Their goals, if they have them, are created without the benefit of carefully examining consequences. This would not be the case if they were properly empowered and helped to understand what it means to be responsible classroom citizens.

Children need to see value in their schooling aside from university preparation and the like. They need to recognize schooling as empowering them for life in the present as well as the future. When the curriculum is too structured and too much control is exercised over students, learning loses its zest. Learning is inherently human, but it must be self-directed in order to be self-sustaining.

High-stakes testing, on the other hand, supports learning that is prescriptive in the extreme and has very little intrinsic value to students. As will be detailed in the next chapter, humans naturally engage in investigations and inquiry as they approach life's problems. Considerable satisfaction is achieved when solutions are found to complex problems through efforts that are encompassed by autonomy.

Empowering students involves the critical issue of whether or not to actively support the development of creativity. As a society we value creativity, while at the same time being fearful of its unchecked manifestations. It is a characteristic that has historically provided the means of advancing society through scientific discoveries as well as art, literature, and so on, while at the same time instilling fear because of the overwhelming need we have to control what happens to us.

Interestingly, because we wish to personally regulate our lives, we are inclined to control the behavior of others, particularly their creativity. In school this obviously reduces opportunities for children to develop their full creative potential. The solution is to empower students by helping them achieve responsible autonomy so they can be trusted while at the same time learning and functioning in a way that promotes creative self-direction.

Life doesn't relate well to excessive structure and standardized tests (Meier, 2002). Yet children are told they must memorize facts and pass these tests to demonstrate their capabilities. Instead, they should be involved in creatively solving problems that are personally relevant. This should be done within a real-life context where students use what they are learning to deal with valid life experiences (Glasser, 1986).

Unfortunately, the legitimacy of any particular interest or skills students may have is inherently determined by whether or not they are included on the tests. This not only limits what is considered valid, it can also reduce the potential success of students in test taking, if their interests are pursued instead of memorizing information to be measured by the tests. In this latter case, students are punished for pursuing personal interests that could have enlivened their school experiences and led to justifiable learning along with the enlargement of personal capacity.

AUTONOMY AS THE BASIS FOR MOTIVATION

Because students typically achieve at levels well below their capability, they rarely acknowledge it as such. They also fail to recognize what is needed to achieve excellence. Consequently, it is unlikely that they will pursue a learning task on their own in order to reach a point of genuine personal fulfillment. Nor will they feel compelled to learn in order to acquire competence. The longer children are in school, the more recalcitrant many become as they cling to low levels of accomplishment. In essence, they become content with mediocrity. It would be a complete surprise for them to discover the thoroughness and effort required to achieve excellence. Many would be even more surprised to learn that they have the inherent capability to attain it.

This state of affairs is due primarily to the common school practice of teachers trying to motivate students to become engaged with assigned learning. Had their learning been driven by their own desires, greater competence could be expected. There is a direct connection between accomplishment and motivation, particularly when students are self-directed (Reeve, 2009). In addition, when they direct their own learning, they become so engaged that they are much less disposed to create discipline problems.

It is unlikely that students will substantially alter the erroneous perceptions of their capabilities by simply having them pointed out. This is because these false conceptions are deeply rooted in individual and group norms (Banks, 2000). Rather the learning environment must be substantially changed. The conditions that lead to misconceptions about quality have to be eliminated. It must become impossible for mediocre performances to be acceptable (Wilkins, 1976).

Children whose shoddy performances have routinely been accepted ordinarily have no plans to alter the quality of their academic accomplishments in the future (Glasser, 1990). They have become comfortable with low quality because nothing else has been expected of them, and because they do not truly appreciate the personal value of what they could accomplish if they properly applied themselves.

In addition, not only do they have no idea how much work would be required, they have limited appreciation of the satisfaction that could be garnered by working as hard as they can and accomplishing great things. In the past, working hard may have meant striving to satisfy others' expectations, which they may have found unsatisfying and even repugnant. To overcome this regretable condition, students must come to know how low performances interfere with satisfying their need for competence. This can only be achieved when they do their very best with learning tasks they help devise and direct in connection with an understanding of what excellence really is.

To be motivated to learn, students depend not only on meeting challenges and demonstrating excellence, but also on making collaborative choices about learning activities (Turner & Meyer, 1995). Choice is an essential part of adolescence. Young people are commonly driven by a desire for increased independence, and when this need is repressed as it often is in school, there is frequently a display of excessive aggressiveness and intolerance (Norton, 1970).

The idea that school children should be permitted to participate individually and collectively in making decisions about curricula and classroom management is not new. It has been advocated for many years and carried out in various schools across the country in an effort to more fully empower children. Despite the fact that self-directed learning is not a particularly novel idea, it has failed to be extensively employed. This is so even though there is considerable support from research for its general application (Eccles et al., 1991).

There are a number of questions regarding student autonomy and empowerment that are too important to be ignored. They have critical implications for student achievement as well as life adjustment. For example, why is it so important for youth to decide what and how they learn? How might greater student autonomy be appropriately provided? What are the barriers to students becoming more self-directed? What can and should be done to eliminate the inappropriate limits commonly placed on student decision making?

Ironically, despite the importance given to life in our democratic society, schools do not properly represent democratic living (Smith, 2001). However, after leaving school, students are expected to assume lives as bonafide participants in democratic communities. It is assumed that they have had the training to do so in school, when in fact the training they have received is more akin to living in a dictatorship. Properly conceived school experiences could be an ideal way for children to learn how to succeed in democratic communities. They could participate with their age-mates, under competent tutelage, in experiences that are a microcosm of life in a democracy. Student empowerment could thus be assured.

Perhaps there is nothing that deprives youth of motivation to learn more than being powerless to regulate themselves (Reeve, 2009). In addition, when facing challenging and difficult situations, having personal autonomy provides a context for them to learn how to face similar situations later in life. When teachers or other school officials exclusively control what goes on in the classroom, students are inclined to shift responsibility to them rather than deal with the problems at hand. In addition, they tend to resist their teachers rather than cooperating. According to Kohn (1993a) self-determination provides at least the five following benefits that contribute to greater motivation and an elevated sense of empowerment.

First, adequate emotional adjustment depends on achieving a strong sense of self-determination. Those who maintain good emotional and physical health sense greater personal control over what happens to them. Fewer conditions lead more reliably to depression and other forms of psychological distress than feeling helpless in consequence of being under the control of others (Seligman, 1995).

Second, responsibility development depends on the presence of self-regulation opportunities. Adults claim they desire children to become more responsible and yet often deny them the very ingredient most essential for this development. To become responsible, children require numerous experiences to practice decision making in an atmosphere of freedom.

Teachers should be completely aware that lack of free choice in the classroom is not only a deterrent to learning responsibility, but it also foments rebellion and stimulates irresponsibility. It appears as if schools don't really value democracy and associated responsibility development, given the controlling tactics routinely employed. In addition, many of the problems most teachers encounter are due to their failure to properly empower children in the classroom. Teachers must frankly admit that the important values associated with democratic living cannot be successfully promoted in the absence of choice (Kohn, 1993a).

Third, motivation to achieve academically depends on having personal autonomy. Students' enthusiasm quickly evaporates in the face of teacher control (Armstrong, 1998). Their waning fervor obviously robs them of potential achievements. The need for self-determination in promoting greater achievement is best illustrated by the eight-year study, in which 30 high schools were encouraged to develop innovative programs that incorporated democratic principles. The students in these schools were followed through high school and college and found to be far more academically successful than their traditionally trained peers. They also exhibited other valuable attitudes at a much higher level (Aiken, 1942).

Student choice motivates students to work more efficiently and effectively on their school work, be more creative, miss less school, score better on national tests of basic skills, have increased reasoning skills, and more persistently study (Kohn, 1993a). The research shows convincingly that motivation and responsible autonomy is a function of being self-directed.

Fourth, sharing decision-making responsibilities with students is a benefit for teachers as well. They report that teaching becomes far more interesting when they collaborate with students about instruction. Of course they have far less need to motivate learning, and perhaps more importantly they discover they have fewer discipline problems. They are able to spend more time interacting with students in positive ways and less time monitoring and correcting their behavior.

Fifth, empowering students with more decision-making opportunities is more consistent with the values to which citizens in a democratic society subscribe. It is also consistent with the way students prefer to be treated and with the way they will be required to interact with others in the communities in which they will eventually live. Thus, it provides teachers with a pattern for authentically relating to their students so as not to compromise basic democratic values. Not only are students more motivated to learn, teachers experience a growing love for teaching. This creates a self-enhancing cycle of teaching and learning that perpetuates high achievement and goodwill.

THE NEED FOR AUTONOMY IN LEARNING

It is self-evident that autonomy is highly valued in a democratic society. In fact the development of responsible autonomy is the goal of all democratic communities because it provides a way of living that is consistent with natural inclinations and promotes the skill and desire to interact constructively with fellow community members. In democratic learning communities, students participate in activities of the mind such as choosing, deciding, deliberating, reflecting, planning, and judging, and develop a complex understanding of how these capabilities relate to democratic living.

Autonomous individuals learn to have both independence from external authority and at the same time mastery of themselves and their own intellectual powers within a social context (DeVries, Hildebrandt, & Zan, 2000). Truly autonomous individuals not only must be free from the dictates and coercive interferences of others, but they must also be free from disabling conflicts within their own personalities that might keep them from using appropriate logic and judgment in decision making (Gibbs, 1979).

It might be helpful to examine how autonomous students are likely to function in a properly organized school situation. The following qualities help define autonomous persons who are also tuned into their roles and responsibility within a democracy. They are adapted from a list created by Dearden (1975).

- Students are encouraged to wonder about things and ask about them with a sense of their right to ask, think about, and justify various events and happenings that could quite naturally be taken for granted. This is done with the purpose of understanding how personal and social implications may interact.
- Students may refuse to agree or comply with what others suggest when these suggestions seem critically unacceptable. However, they seek to understand the views of others and how they compare with their own and value others' input as much as their own.
- Students define what is wanted or is in their personal best interest, as distinct from what may be conventionally accepted, and compare this with the needs and desires of all group members. Group requirements are considered to be just as important as personal desires.
- Students conceive of personal goals, policies, and plans in connection with the wishes of other group members. They are cognizant of the problems associated with anyone in the group, including themselves, imposing their will on others to obtain compliance.
- Students choose among alternative proposals and ideas, making deliberate choices consistent with personal and group purposes.
- Students form personal opinions on various topics of interest and compare their positions with other students. They become astute in judging and comparing various points of view and determining their relative merits.
- Students govern their behavior and attitudes through a process of personal and group decision making, based on careful consideration of principles and ideals that are acceptable to the individual and the group.

Autonomous persons must not only be free from others' coercive influence, but must also be free from personal compulsions and rigidities. Autonomy requires responsiveness to others and an ability to make creative, unique responses to situations that take others' views into account, but which do not arise from stereotypical responses that are connected to previous experiences of forced compliance. Mature autonomy is characterized by individuals who are free from continual and pressing needs for reassurance and approval from others and by the ability to skillfully and independently solve problems. At the same time, these individuals relish interdependence and recognize that one receives benefits from society by contributing to it and that personal rights always have a corollary social responsibility (Chickering, 1969).

To develop responsible autonomy, students should be involved in learning activities that involve their peers. Group projects should replace the current practice of children mostly working in isolation. Responsible autonomy cannot exist apart from interactions with others. Within a democracy, autonomy always contains social components. Students need to coordinate their views with others to achieve a higher level of personal understanding and satisfaction.

Children become more able decision makers if they develop intellectually within group settings. In social settings they are confronted with greater complexity as they compare their views with classmates, analyze situations, and make assessments of various ideas and explanations. It is good life preparation, because as adults much problem solving is done in group settings.

Children should be encouraged to compare their ideas with classmates because it provides them an opportunity to think critically and make more complicated assessments and comparisons. This kind of activity also encourages students to modify their ideas and conclusions when it is clear that the ideas of their peers are more defensible. Students should be allowed to make assessments of all kinds of ideas, including wrong ones. Only when all ideas are respected and given serious consideration can children develop intellectual and moral autonomy (Noddings, 2002).

In promoting autonomy, it is essential for students to validly assess their own thinking without incrimination. They should be free of derogatory statements by peers or teachers. In addition, they should try to address problems that do not have only one right answer. There should be allowance for genuine differences of opinion about these matters.

Even if only a single right answer applies, students should present their current thinking with the knowledge that their expressions are tentative. Their contributions are subject to change at any time without the possibility of any negative reactions being made. Consequently, faulty ideas are subject to change without unfavorable comments and with little or no finality being attached to them. This kind of discussion provides a time to exchange ideas and build an understanding of various issues, with the premise that making modifications in thinking can be anticipated as the norm.

EMPOWERING STUDENTS IN MORAL LEARNING COMMUNITIES

Because teachers have the ultimate authority for what happens in the classroom, schools constitute a particularly difficult environment for students to learn how to function successfully in democratic learning communities. This authority cannot simply be passed on to students without regard to questionable student behavior. At the same time, teachers should not employ their authority in heavy-handed ways, depriving students of the freedom necessary for growth and development in a democratic society. Again, teachers must learn to balance necessary restrictions with gradually empowering students to the greatest extent possible, given their degree of growth in judgment and responsible decision making.

Undoubtedly authority will always be vested in educators who have the responsibility to provide instructional leadership. But teachers must not assume that such authority makes it necessary for them to define all learning activities and take responsibility for all student achievement. For students to become empowered, responsible learners, more decision making must eventually be transferred to them. The purpose of authority in learning communities is not to exercise rigid control over students and direct all learning. Instead authority should be defined as the leadership required to help students increasingly direct their own learning and achieve higher levels of excellence than is possible under the strict control of teachers.

Because students guard their freedom jealously and resist their teachers when personal freedom is at risk, teachers must share decision-making responsibilities in the classroom with them. Students may begrudgingly forfeit freedom when they see no alternative, but they don't simply capitulate and then engage in effective learning. They are more likely to devote less time and energy to learning themselves and to sabotage the efforts of classmates. It is, therefore, essential for teachers to promote better student decision making, group cohesiveness, helpfulness, and social responsibility so that students don't feel pressured to simply conform to teacher expectations.

Students require sufficient independence from authority in order to master themselves and learn to direct their own thinking and decision making. Without this kind of instruction they are unlikely to develop the skills of choosing, deciding, deliberating, reflecting, and judging and are consequently hampered in learning the essentials of living in democratic communities.

Autonomous persons are able to function both independently and as integrated members of learning communities. As group members they provide important contributions to group interactions and enhance growth promoting interdependence. They develop well-orchestrated contributions that incorporate personal goals and desires with related social responsibility.

In order to become strong group members, students must be taught to promote their personal points of view without backing down prematurely and to create their own views and goals, which they can capably defend and expertly implement. At the same time, they must be sensitive to the views of other members of the group and learn that personal autonomy is inextricably connected to successful social discourse and action. Teachers must help students stay focused on thoughtful, independent actions that enhance group growth and development and learn that the satisfaction of personal needs can only be achieved through responsible group participation.

Teachers should realize that students work with greater commitment toward collective goals than individual ones (Csikszentmihalyi, 1990). Learning communities provide a powerful way in which to increase both need satisfaction and commitment to learning. In the process students become responsible persons with little inclination to disrupt teaching and learning. Instead they are disposed to ensure that the classroom environment is conducive to effective learning.

Chapter Four

Democratic Discipline and Learning Motivation

Highly motivated students are rarely disruptive in the classroom. Not only are they less likely to interfere with the learning of their peers, they also demand a more learner-friendly classroom atmosphere for themselves. Because learning in democratic communities is primarily influenced by intrinsic motivation, students have a vested interest in making sure there is an appropriate learning environment. The result is students not only being motivated to learn, but also helping ensure that the classroom atmosphere is conducive to learning for everyone.

In most teacher training programs, prospective teachers are taught how to motivate students. It is assumed that students are not self-motivated and thus must be supplied with reasons to study by the teacher. It is thus inferred that students consider learning an aversive activity. This is often true when it comes to school learning, but it is not true for learning generally. Human beings are intrinsically interested in learning from early childhood through adulthood.

It is true that some students do find learning in school to be aversive, but even these students routinely spend time learning and enjoying it outside the school setting. It can't be said that they are not motivated to learn. Rather, they are not motivated to learn what is offered in school. Teachers are apparently unable to routinely supply learning activities that are sufficiently motivating to keep them enthusiastically involved.

Toddlers spend much of their day engaged in learning. They seem driven to understand and master their environment (Piaget, 1954). They can't be kept from it. Adults are also commonly intrinsically motivated to spend considerable time learning about the world in which they live. Learning interests are so varied among adults that it is tempting to say that only some of them are consistently involved in learning what is ordinarily considered worthwhile. For example, there may only be a few adults involved in reading books which society would accept as truly educational. But this may be associated more with the advent of television and the Internet than just a disinterest in reading.

Even young children spend many hours on the Internet. The question may be raised regarding the value of what is learned there. But the same issue can be raised regarding what is learned in school. The fact that many children are not motivated to learn what schools offer constitutes a sufficient reason to investigate the school curricula to determine its true value rather than just assuming that the school offerings are unquestionably superior to other options and that children must be motivated to learn it if they are not already so inclined.

Also, just because students are not learning much in school, it can't be concluded that they have to be extrinsically motivated in order to learn what is considered by educators to be of most worth. And it can't be concluded that the concepts and skills that are interesting to children outside the school curriculum are of little worth. What students prefer to learn should not simply be discounted because it is not part of school offerings.

The fact that various officials have designated particular curricular content as required learning doesn't somehow sanctify it and prove conclusively that what is required is without a doubt the most valuable and appropriate learning. The same can also be asserted regarding the nature of the learning process. There have been disagreements historically about school curricula, and such differences of opinion continue to manifest themselves presently.

When it comes to motivation, educators need to be more broad minded and study the subject carefully. The nature of the curriculum, along with the process of motivation, should be carefully examined and insights applied to help drive the learning process. It might be well for a balance to be struck between what children find inherently interesting and what society considers to be most important.

Simply discounting intrinsic motivation because student choices may not be completely consistent with the prescribed curriculum or teachers' expectations is very short-sighted. The educational process is far better served by teachers who attempt to capitalize on intrinsic motivation as appropriate and motivate in other ways where it seems justified. Emphasizing intrinsic motivation doesn't mean that students should be allowed to learn whatever they want. Rather, teachers should try to understand the natural motivation process and integrate it into the curriculum, deferring to extrinsic motivation only when it is provided in appropriate ways.

When teachers employ extrinsic rewards to promote learning, they commonly base their efforts on the expectancy-value theory, which indicates that the effort students are willing to make to learn what they are assigned by their teachers depends on the degree to which they think they will be able to learn successfully, and whether they will feel satisfied with their endeavors. Students are unlikely to apply themselves in school when there are neither intrinsic nor extrinsic outcomes they value. They also tend to be put off learning even highly valued knowledge if they believe they cannot be successful no matter how hard they try (Good & Brophy, 2000). People's efforts are thus governed by what is referred to as attribution theory.

Attribution theory indicates that people are motivated by the hope that they will achieve understanding and master the environment and themselves. This is the main instigator of behavior. All individuals are in fact naive scientists, trying to understand their environment and, in particular, trying to comprehend the casual determinants of their behavior as well as the behavior of others. Thus, they try to understand why things happen (Pintrich & Schunk, 1996).

Attributions depend on individual perception. Consequently, if almost everyone succeeded on a task, it is likely to be considered easy. But if most people failed, it would be considered hard. In contrast, when an individual succeeds when most people fail or fails when most people succeed, it is attributed to the individual's personal capabilities (Werner, 1990).

People can make incorrect inferences that lead to biases as they make attributions regarding potential success. Errors include:

- Attributing actions of others to dispositional or personal factors and ignoring situational factors that might be partially or even more causally related to the behavior.
- Making attributions that are biased by the person being in the situation themselves.
- Making attributions that reflect biases, ego-defensiveness, or self-protective biases.
- Taking more credit for an outcome than appropriate, regardless of the actual success or failure.
- Responding as it is believed other people would respond in the same situation (Pintrich & Schunk, 1996).

It is essential to note that there are sex differences in achievement attribution that appear as early as age four. The same differences exist in adults as well and can be linked to sex role stereotypes in which higher competence is commonly ascribed to males. Girls' attributions may prevent them from having confidence in their own ability and fail to help them learn how to cope effectively with failure. Elementary school teachers are likely to have the same attribution characteristics and, therefore, be inclined to reinforce those held by children as they enter school (Lochel, 1983).

THE NATURE OF PERSONAL INTERESTS

It is the usual routine for teachers to require their students to engage in common learning activities. This is justified by what is thought to be best for them. At least this is the usual defense made, and it is supposedly warranted because of the curricular decisions made at various levels of government. Teachers also defend such tactics because they consider common learning experiences to be easier to create and manage and less likely to promote discipline problems. It is also assumed that less preparation time is required, along with greater accuracy in measuring student achievement.

However, educators must carefully examine these assumptions and methods to see if they are justified when compared to practices that employ student interests and inclinations. Unfortunately student interests have not been carefully studied to determine the extent to which they are consistent with what society values. It is simply assumed that they lack sufficient experience and understanding to be involved in making such decisions.

By the same token, educators and others have not consistently studied school offerings to determine how to get them to map onto student interests. Student interests are simply ignored because they are generally considered irrelevant to what educators believe is important for them to learn. This is usually done without considering that there might be some compatibility between them. The enlightened use of intrinsic motivation is thus excluded while the benefit it could serve in motivating students and reducing the incidence of discipline problems fails to be considered. In consequence of this, students are denied opportunities to develop responsible self-direction, which is essential to their growth and development as they prepare to occupy a personal niche in bonafide democratic communities throughout their lives.

Even toddlers appear to inherently engage in daily activities in a very personal way and follow their idiosyncratic interests in a most compelling fashion. Thwarting their self-directed play often promotes discord in the form of tantrums. In addition, toddlers don't require adults to encourage them to engage in learning, particularly if they are allowed to pursue their own agendas. They direct personal learning quests with considerable intensity without adult intervention.

As they get older, many children interrogate adults in an effort to obtain a greater understanding of the world in which they live. Often their search is a futile one. Parents may be unprepared or reluctant to share sufficient time with children to fully answer their questions. In addition, they are unlikely to create an environment that stimulates a quest for learning. Also, teachers ordinarily don't have sufficient time to help individual children explore their questions. They are too busy managing the common learning activities and discipline issues normally faced each day.

Moreover, even if they are inclined to do so, teachers usually limit their responsibility to answering children's questions so far as they are able, rather than seeing students' questions as expressions of their sincere interests that could be used to help guide instruction. They rarely use such questioning episodes to help children explore their queries in a meaningful way or engage in significant research. Ordinarily they consider themselves to be too busy, or they may be too enamored with the predesignated curricula to entertain learning quests that don't map directly onto their instructional plans. In the classroom, the result is for children to abandon their inquiries in favor of simply responding to teachers' questions, even though they have far less interest in them than in following their own curiosities.

The No Child Left Behind Act only intensified this problem. When children's interests get derailed, they don't automatically become interested in activities designated by their teachers. Rather, they are more likely to interact with their peers or anticipate activities which take place outside the classroom, like athletic competition, music performances, and debate contests. Sometimes remaining eligible to engage in these activities may be the only inducement that encourages them to perform as teachers direct. It is interesting that eligibility for extracurricular activities is made contingent on classroom performances. These restrictions technically constitute negative reinforcement with a punitive countenance and illustrate the coercive mindset of many educators.

Instead of always expecting children to abandon their interests while trying to figure out how to get them to follow teacher directions, it seems more reasonable to let students' interests help shape the curriculum. This can be pursued in a more appropriate way if teachers anticipate that at least some of their students will want to learn what they consider legitimate subjects, while at the same time not assuming that students have nothing to offer.

Even if some students want to engage in learning activities that teachers judge to be of little value, it may be wise to let them instead of suffering student boredom or discipline problems. It is possible that such learning activities may eventually prove to be valuable, particularly when teachers skillfully help students build upon their initial interests and become involved in more productive learning. At the very least, students may learn something about directing their own learning. Afterward they may be asked to assess their efforts and determine if their projects were worthwhile.

This doesn't mean that teachers should allow students to do whatever they wish all the time. Instead, it provides a framework for teachers to start with students' interests and gradually help them reframe their learning inclinations as they come to see more appropriate and promising avenues to follow. Skillful teachers help their students to see new, unfamiliar possibilities as they become involved in following their own interests. These teachers can extend student learning to include activities that they find interesting, but that also map onto what teachers believe is critical.

Many times, useful learning activities are simply things students haven't thought of but that students become interested in when introduced to them. Students need to feel that they are trusted and empowered to make important decisions about what they learn. Only in this way can sufficient student commitment be expected. Teachers should ask themselves, "Is it better to force students to comply with prescribed learning activities and consequently get very little from them or to have them productively involved with experiences that may be different from what is ordinarily expected, and perhaps a little tangent to what teachers feel is fully acceptable, and have them pursue these with vigor?"

Obviously, what is studied should fit the particular course subject to some degree. There are likely many topics for study associated with a particular school subject that the teacher or other entities may not consider as important as other possibilities. Often these topics are in reality legitimate areas of study that can be fully justified for inclusion in the curriculum. It makes little sense to so constrain a subject that little latitude is permitted, particularly when there is no real necessity for such constraint aside from the preferences of those who select topics for study.

Manifestly, there are some concepts in any field of knowledge that are central to a proper understanding, but there is also a lot of information in the prescribed curriculum that could justifiably be replaced by other concepts. When more options are available within a context of offering students more say regarding what they learn, greater commitment and achievement are realized. At the same time, there is hardly anything that is lost by such an approach, particularly when considering what children actually remember from the prescribed curriculum that they are asked to commit to memory. Students forget more than half of the meaningful conceptual information taught in school within a period of six weeks, with more dimming of recall in subsequent days (Cronbach, 1963).

Many students do not have a clear conception of their specific interests in various aspects of a subject. They simply do not have enough experience with these subjects to make this kind of determination. Thus it is correct to assume that many students don't have intrinsic interests in the courses they take. In many instances, participation in these learning experiences is a requirement. At the same time, students are likely to be motivated by helping to make decisions about what and how they learn. Consequently, students need to acquire a greater understanding about various possible options they could pursue.

Usually teachers just launch into the various topics without properly introducing them to their students and showing them different alternative aspects of various subjects. To properly capitalize on the need students have to be self-directed, teachers could present a broad spectrum of possible topics that could be studied while at the same time showing students possible implications for studying each of these.

At the same time, potential learning strategies could be suggested along with some general descriptions regarding key concepts. Students could be told how to make decisions about what they learn. For example, curiosity, usefulness for practical living, or preparation for college attendance could all be used by students to help determine the curriculum. In a democratic learning community these initial topics are used as springboards into more in-depth, self-initiated studies.

EMPLOYING MOTIVATION

Because it is best for students to anticipate success with reasonable effort, teachers face the challenge of encouraging students to engage in learning at an appropriate level of difficulty. Here again students are likely to have a wide range of what they consider challenging and, therefore, need to engage in learning at a level that is sufficiently comfortable, but that allows them to achieve excellence. Teachers should recognize that students' perceptions of how difficult a learning task is helps to determine the extent of their motivation. If it is too easy, they never really achieve an appropriate level of satisfaction. If it is too hard, they may give up without trying.

Learning that is too easy is usually considered by students to be busy-work, but some tasks may be so complex and difficult that even the most talented students cannot anticipate success. Students need their teachers to help them learn to make appropriate choices regarding how challenging a proposed area of study may be. A suitable level of difficulty exists when students understand what to do and how to do it well enough to achieve a high level of success if they persistently employ suitable strategies (Good & Brophy, 2000). This helps students concentrate on learning without worrying about failure (Blumenfeld, Puro, & Mergendoller, 1992).

Teachers must be wary of defining the relative difficulty of students' academic work as essentially the same for all. That is because each student's perception of the degree of difficulty can be remarkably different from that of peers. In addition, children have differences in abilities that must be taken into account. Also, their perceptions are likely to depend on past successes or failures. Students who have previously experienced failure are likely to undersell their capabilities. This cannot be quickly quelled by teachers offering reassurance or providing contrived success experiences. Strategies for helping students overcome the low estimate of their capabilities are detailed later in the chapter in a discussion regarding attribution retraining.

In trying to help students learn to accommodate themselves to appropriate levels of difficulty, teachers must teach them to make valid assessments based on experience. Otherwise some students may overestimate the difficulty of learning tasks and habitually perform well below their capabilities, while others may be unsuccessful because they have underestimated the difficulty of what they set out to learn.

Also teachers need to inform their students that they can drastically increase their accomplishments through increased efforts. However, they have to be careful not to raise expectations beyond what they can adequately achieve. This can cause students' expectations to spiral up until they can no longer accomplish what they wish and eventually suffer consequent self-concept problems (Covington & Beery, 1976).

Perhaps the easiest way to achieve a comfortable level of difficulty is for students to personally determine the kind of learning tasks they feel prepared for, with the stipulation that they should periodically make assessments upon which any adjustments can be based. This has the added benefit of providing greater incentives for students. Under these conditions, students are more likely to stretch themselves and enthusiastically learn, but to do so in a reasonable way.

Students are unlikely to achieve success in school unless they have a valid view of personal capacity. When students view themselves as capable, they are much more likely to succeed. When students see themselves as adequate learners and believe success is within their reach, they will be more highly motivated. They will consequently expend more effort and exhibit greater persistence.

This occurs more readily when students set goals of moderate difficulty, seriously commit themselves to pursuing these goals, and concentrate on trying to achieve success rather than avoid failure (Dweck & Elliott, 1983). Students work harder when they see themselves as competent and capable of achieving success (Bandura, 1997) and in the process they do better when they attribute their effectiveness to their own initiative and capabilities rather than outside factors (Weiner, 1992).

RESILIENCY TRAINING

One of the most important attributes children can acquire in life is resilience. This is the ability to encounter problems with a sense of equanimity and avoid experiencing trauma, helplessness, and depression. Resilient people routinely bounce back from the deleterious effects of hazardous or traumatic situations through problem solving rather than giving up when facing harm and potential failure. This is particularly important when they confront life's problems. Even the encounters students commonly have in school classrooms can require they be bolstered with resilience. It has been found that resilient people are able to face usually difficult situations without resorting to violence or despair. Rather, they meet challenges with poise.

Researchers have discovered that between one-half and two-thirds of children who grow up in families with mentally disturbed members, who have parents who are alcoholic, abusive, or criminally involved, or who live in poverty-stricken or war-torn communities seem able to adjust to potentially damaging conditions with resilience. This is in part due to an inborn capacity for resilience, which provides a way to develop social competence, problem-solving abilities, a critical consciousness, autonomy, and an innate sense of purpose (Werner & Smith, 1989).

Resilience is also due to the presence of protective factors in the individual's environment that provide an ambience for optimal growth. These include caring relationships, high expectations, and opportunities to participate meaningfully within the communities where they live (Benard, 1993). When these are not acquired at home, schools become a logical place to provide them.

The development of resilience is associated with high expectations. When students have high expectations of themselves, they perform better and develop more positive views of themselves. This is particularly true when they are involved in defining the excellence to which they aspire. Students who have meaningful relationships with teachers and peers and are truly appreciated for who they are, along with being successful in their academic endeavors, take on a persona of having contributions to make (Rutter, 1979).

Instead of feeling incompetent and alienated, resilient people sense personal empowerment. They become inclined to assume personal responsibility for themselves and acquire a greater sense of purpose and personal commitment (Sarason, 1990). These attributes help them to assume a more active role in learning communities and enter into more caring relationships with their associates.

To acquire protective resilience, students should be more meaningfully involved in problem solving and decision making and in helping their peers and teachers create instructional goals (Fox, 1994). They need to help make choices about the instructional program and the means to be used for evaluating their learning. Otherwise, their personal well-being is sacrificed (Benard, 1993). When they are personally involved in defining curricula, they are able to perceive relevance and acquire a sense of personal responsibility and ownership. Also, when caring relationships are fostered along with intellectual growth, the desperation and loneliness that many adolescents feel can be thwarted (Phelan, Davidson, & Cao, 1992).

For some students the only hope of being accepted and appreciated, and in the process developing resilience, depends on the elimination of the usual adversarial associations they experience in traditional schools and the formation of learning communities that foster the kind of caring necessary to combat these negative influences. Unfortunately schools inherently create adversarial conditions, which even astute teachers may have difficulty countering (Darling-Hammond, 1997).

Optimism is an essential ingredient of resilience. Without optimism, depression often develops. Teachers should be aware that optimism does not come from being told positive things, or from having images of victory during competition, but rather from thinking about causes of success in particular ways. There are three critical dimensions children always use to explain why any particular good or bad consequence occurs: permanence, pervasiveness, and personalization (Seligman, 1995).

Pessimistic people believe that the bad things that happen to them are permanent, that nothing can change what has occurred. From this perspective, bad things happen perpetually with no way of escaping them. They use such sullen terms as *never*, *always*, and *no matter what* to describe adverse events in their lives.

Optimistic individuals, on the other hand, see bad events as temporary and amenable to modification. They resist the threat of depression by routinely concluding that they will eventually recover from setbacks and that problems can be eventually solved. They not only believe that problems are temporary and can be altered with personal effort, but also that there are high and low points in life, and that the highs can be magnified and lows minimized. Optimistic youngsters consistently explain good events in terms of their permanence. They routinely focus on possessing such positive traits as being a hard worker or being likeable. These they see as being under their control and permanent.

Pessimistic people tend to have an external locus of control and consequently attribute their success to luck or fate, while optimistic individuals have an internal locus of control and believe their success is a function of effort and planning. When children see their success or failure as being within their control, they routinely assume that they can be successful if they practice more or modify their approach in some way, even though they have initially failed at some task.

When failure is attributed to personal ability, luck, or the difficulty of the task, however, students assume they have less power over what happens to them and believe that making greater effort or organizing their endeavors will have little effect on what they can accomplish (Smith & Price, 1996). Unfortunately, modifying an external locus of control is difficult, particularly in a school setting where in all likelihood this frame of reference grew in the first place. It is insightful to realize that this perspective primarily comes from the practice of teachers exclusively assessing student achievement.

When students have little or no role in assessing their own achievements, no amount of praise or providing them artificially contrived success experiences is likely to alter their opinions. Rather, students with an external locus of control must be taught how to make self-assessments that are credible. This is not a simple matter because nearly all students have been evaluated exclusively by their teachers. They have no basis upon which to judge their performances.

Because they have routinely been provided grades by their teachers, and because high grades are considered essential and thus prized by students, they are likely to evaluate themselves in terms of desired grades and inflate their assessments. To wean them from these inaccurate perceptions, students should learn to make comparative appraisals of their work in which they have engaged in better planning and made greater efforts than previously. They will eventually learn that effort and planning can in fact improve their work.

Pervasiveness is the practice of students projecting causes and effects across many situations. While optimistic children see their success as predictable from one kind of activity to another, their pessimistic counterparts use global explanations for their failure and give up. They anticipate failing even before they've begun. For example, pessimistic individuals may conclude from poor golf scores that they are bad in all sports.

Optimistic persons, on the other hand, may admit they don't do well at golf and not include other sports in this declaration. Optimistic children usually think globally about positive attributes and incidents. When a high grade is received in physics, optimistic children conclude that they are smart rather than reserving their positive assessment only to physics, as is the case with pessimistic people.

Personalization is the third way for explaining how good or bad events happen. In this case, the individual tries to determine who is at fault for various occurrences. If something bad happens, children can blame themselves, other people, or the circumstances surrounding the event. Individuals who blame themselves when they fail ordinarily suffer low self-esteem. On the other hand, those who blame other people or circumstances for their failures should be taught to hold themselves accountable and encouraged to rectify the situation and determine how to avoid having them repeated in the future.

Children need to see themselves realistically so they can take responsibility for problems they cause. It is particularly critical for them to learn that they can often predict problems and alter circumstances in order to avoid failure. They must fully understand that they can effectively solve problems if they have sufficient time and make an adequate effort.

Seligman (1995) has concluded that traditional efforts made to protect the self-concepts of children are responsible for a rising tide of depression that has occurred in society over the past six or seven decades. Fearing that children's self-concepts can be damaged by failure, teachers and parents often move to soften their expectations. Children are thus shielded from experiences and consequences that ordinarily would have strengthened them and helped them avoid depression. The real culprit is accepting mediocre student performances as acceptable and approving of student work that is far below the quality of which they are capable.

It is commonly feared that dire consequences will occur unless students' feelings of anger, sadness, and anxiety are cushioned. However, these feelings help motivate them to make the necessary adaptations in order to accomplish their goals. Rather than depression being the result of facing difficult situations, it comes about by avoiding them and in the process failing to achieve one's goals.

When children confront problems, if parents or teachers try to modify the situation to help bolster self-esteem, moderate the difficulties, and distract them with distortions of what is required for real success, it becomes harder for children to actually test their limits and achieve the best of which they are capable. Unfortunately, when they are deprived of excellence, their self-esteem is weakened as it would be had they been belittled, humiliated, and physically thwarted at every turn (Seligman, 1995).

Rather than exposing children to contrived success experiences or praising mediocre student performances, teachers should help children understand the nature of excellence and show them how to achieve it. This, they should learn, takes time and effort and more thoughtful approaches to learning. A greater sense of resiliency will be the result.

Children with resiliency are able to handle frustrating, difficult situations with equanimity. They are also unlikely to be disruptive in class or get so upset that they resort to violence. In connection with this, it has been shown that caring relationships, high expectations, and opportunities to participate in learning communities promotes resilience, which in turn shields children from depression (Benard, 1993). Thus, the conditions that in the past teachers feared would cause depression in reality prepare children to avoid this malady.

EXTRINSIC MOTIVATION

It is commonly concluded by educators that rewarding students for their efforts in school automatically produces greater efforts and higher achievement. However, research has uncovered a darker side to this practice. For example, the more rewards are used, the more they seem to be needed (Kohn, 1993b). Children who initially may be inclined to learn without rewards may afterward refuse to learn without them. Learning that ordinarily is driven by intrinsic motivation may require an extrinsic reward once a reinforcement program is instituted.

Interestingly, children who receive extrinsic rewards eventually hate what they have to do to get them (Deci, 1981; Lepper, 1983). Of course, in school this involves learning. It has also been shown that controlling instruction with reinforcers on one task reduces students' interest in subsequent tasks. Apparently the motivation-killing features of control can spill over to adversely affect attitudes about new learning activities (Enzle & Wright, 1992). Ironically, merely watching someone else being reinforced can have a motivation-killing effect (Morgan, 1983).

Rewards also affect the quality of the work individuals do. Professional artists do less creative work when it is contracted for in advance for a specified reward (Amabile, 1992). Students use less sophisticated learning strategies when they are rewarded. Also, only very simple—indeed mindless—tasks are improved when they are rewarded (Kohn, 1993b). People who are given rewards choose easier tasks, are less efficient in using available information to solve novel problems, and tend to be answer oriented and more illogical in their problem-solving strategies than intrinsically motivated people (Condry, 1977).

It should be pointed out that this negative scenario does not apply in all conditions. During the 1970s and 1980s research initially indicated that extrinsic reinforcement simply undermined intrinsic motivation. However, it was later discovered that this was only true when students were offered rewards that they knew were designed to pressure them into responding as directed. This included behavior that was being carefully monitored, required to avoid punishment, compared to classmates, and under the pressure of meeting time deadlines (Kohn, 1993b; Lepper, 1983). The thing that undermines intrinsic motivation is offering rewards as incentives in advance of what is expected and following through in ways that make students believe that the reason for any particular behavior was to earn the rewards, not because learning had value in its own right.

Offering rewards in order to stimulate achievement is a far more complex process than many teachers assume. They should recognize that rewards adversely affect intrinsic motivation when they are very attractive and presented in ways that call attention to them, when they are given for just participating in learning activities rather than for achieving specific goals, and when they have obvious control connotations rather than being a natural outcome of learning (Brophy, 1998).

In order to avoid undermining intrinsic motivation, teachers can provide unannounced rewards so that they are seen as expressions of appreciation rather than as a payment of promised incentives. They can also use rewards as feedback on learning activities rather than as control mechanisms. Finally, teachers can provide rewards not merely for participating in activities, but for accomplishing important personal goals (Cameron & Pierce, 1994, 1996; Chance, 1993).

In addition, it is wise if teachers are more discriminating about the kinds of learning activities they reward extrinsically. For example, rewards are more effective at increasing the intensity of student effort than improving the quality of performance. Consequently it is better to supply rewards for routine tasks instead of novel ones, intentional learning rather than incidental learning or discovery activities, and tasks that can be quantified rather than those involving analytical thinking, creativity, artistry, or craftsmanship.

Thus, extrinsic rewards are effective in learning routine computations, practicing musical scales, typing, spelling, shooting free throws, and naming the parts of the human skeleton, but less effective for activities teachers prefer that children do on their own like watching educational television, reading good books, participating in research projects, painting, sculpting, writing creative papers, or participating in community activities such as attending city council meetings, visiting nursing homes, or participating in environmental study groups and clean-up efforts.

Teachers must be wary of providing rewards as incentives. Instead, the importance of learning should be emphasized along with helping students recognize the quality of school work that verifies excellence (Brophy, 1998). Unfortunately most of the rewards provided to students by their teachers, including grades, are given as incentives and suffer from the problems already mentioned.

Discriminating teachers promote learning in ways that reflect an understanding of the implications of various motivation strategies. They particularly understand how various forms of motivation influence self-regulation. Although pursuit of extrinsic rewards can be consistent with self-regulation, it rarely is. Usually rewards are used in ways that override self-regulation. With a strong emphasis on rewards, the basis upon which individuals regulate and maintain growth and a sense of connectedness is being unwittingly supplanted by a reliance on externally imposed incentives, which makes people act in ways incongruent with their needs and self-regulatory tendencies (Ryan & Deci, 2000b).

In addition, it has been learned that motivating children with rewards is far more complex than earlier believed. Effectiveness depends on the nature of the activity, the feedback obtained, the general context for reward administration, and the people offering and receiving the reward. For many children the effectiveness of reinforcers depends on acquiring competence. However, each student may have their own definition of competence. Thus, each individual may be motivated in different ways depending on how he or she defines a learning activity. Put simply, there are individual differences regarding how students respond to both intrinsic and extrinsic motivation (Sansone & Harackiewicz, 2000).

Yet is has been shown that intrinsic motivation is positively related to perceived competence and internal control while perceived lack of control is associated with learned helplessness. Because intrinsic motivation is encouraged by challenge, curiosity, personal control, and fantasy, it behooves educators to plan instruction accordingly and carefully monitor its effects on their students' motivation (Pintrich & Schunk, 1996).

In an effort to encourage student learning, teachers commonly offer praise. Here again it is important to understand the implications of inappropriately praising student performances. When student achievement is praised, there is a tendency for students to view personal acceptance by teachers as conditional. Thus, students may feel they are only acceptable when they achieve what teachers propose. In the process, they may be robbed of independence, creative growth, and even a sense of well-being. Self-concept problems are often a consequence of supposed conditional acceptance created by praising children's achievements. In addition, some students find it embarrassing to be singled out and praised. It may cast them in a role as an "apple polisher" and be aversive to them rather than rewarding.

It has also been found that praise can greatly diminish inquiry behavior. This occurs when teachers habitually employ a particular sequence of responses following students' answers to questions. If students correctly answers a question, teachers usually mimic the answer given and then follow this up with praise. For example, the teacher may ask, "What is the capital of Idaho?" If the student makes the correct response of "Boise," the teacher says, "Boise, that is correct. Good response, Amy." This practice not only eliminates student inquiry, but it also limits the length and thoughtfulness of their responses. It turns teaching into recitation sessions (Edwards & Surma, 1980).

Many times teachers create competitive activities in an effort to motivate students, and of course grading is the most pervasive form of competition in schools. Despite the almost universal use of grades, teachers should understand important implications for this practice. First, competition distracts students from learning. In a competitive environment, students become so focused on getting good grades or winning that they pay little or no attention to what they are learning and consequently value learning less and are less able to visualize how to improve their performances (Ames & Ames, 1981).

Second, competition may enhance performance on routine, simple tasks, but it becomes a distraction when students engage in discovery learning or creativity. It should be added that competition is effective only when all competitors have an equal chance of winning. However, in the grading scheme, with its sorting purposes, a whole spectrum of grades is dictated. It is inconceivable that students actually believe they have an equal chance of receiving high grades.

Third, in competition, there must be losers as well as winners. Often competition is thought of in positive terms because winners are produced. However, there must also be losers. These individuals become the chaff of the grading system. They not only receive little recognition, their achievements are not valued even though they may be the best the individual can offer.

Students who receive low grades are the casualties of schooling. They routinely suffer permanent loss of confidence, self-concept, and enjoyment of school. Usually they lower expectations of themselves and their achievements plummet. All this is justified in the name of determining who is fit for further schooling (Epstein & Harackiewicz, 1992; Moriarty, Douglas, Punch, & Hattie, 1995; Reeve & Deci, 1996).

INTRINSIC MOTIVATION

When an educational experience is valued by the learner because it carries personal meaning or because it is viewed as instrumental in accomplishing something important to the individual, we say he or she is intrinsically motivated. Unfortunately intrinsic motivation has been almost exclusively associated with recreational activities, while learning has been defined as hard and commonly unpleasant work, and affiliated with extrinsic rewards.

Educators teach as though learning is unpleasant and thus requires enticing rewards to induce participation. On the contrary, however, there are aspects of learning that children do find intrinsically motivating. Sometimes they have an inherent interest in a particular topic or they may find some things they learn to be useful in accomplishing desired goals. In addition, students find some learning experiences motivating because they increase their competence in a recognizable way. This kind of motivation is particularly potent when learning is self-directed and students are able to achieve a high level of excellence, as is the case in learning communities.

Intrinsic motivation is connected to human needs and desires. We all have a desire for self-regulation, affection and acceptance, fun, and freedom from external control (Glasser, 1984). We also have a need for creative expression, satisfying curiosity, and exploration, all of which, if they are properly applied to curriculum construction, can help children satisfy their needs along with allowing them to participate in valid educational experiences.

Intrinsically rewarding, self-determined learning tends to be of higher quality than extrinsically motivated learning (Deci & Ryan, 1994). Children want to achieve competence so that they can successfully control complex, critical environmental factors that directly influence how well they can meet their needs. In order to accomplish this, each individual engages in such activities as self-directed exploration, thought, and play (White, 1959).

Intrinsic motivation is devoid of external prods, promises, or threats. Intrinsically motivated students engage in learning activities for their own sake, not for an externally imposed goal. Personal, idiosyncratic interests make it unnecessary to impose pressure to learn (Deci & Ryan, 1994). Learning communities are specifically created to take advantage of students' intrinsic interests. This is done by students being involved in discussing potential learning projects and helping to make decisions about what they learn. Usually these projects are inquiry based and involve a number of students working cooperatively together.

When students' intrinsic interests are honored by their teachers in learning communities, they are much more inclined to not only responsibly regulate their own learning, but to also forthrightly help prevent discipline problems. With more freedom, they are more inclined to be helpful and cooperative rather than disruptive and rebellious.

In learning communities, not only is the instructional program thoughtfully created, appropriate attitudes regarding discipline are also fostered. As more self-regulated learning activities are employed, students become more inclined toward responsible self-determination. They do not require prodding to perform, but rather experience dissatisfaction if they fail to do their best. Intrinsic motivation depends essentially on the degree of autonomy students have. They are not intrinsically motivated if their learning is excessively managed.

Learning communities provide an excellent format for promoting intrinsic motivation because they are designed to satisfy students' needs for autonomy, competence, and relatedness. Intrinsic motivation is stimulated when students are able to function effectively in a social setting, particularly when they acquire a valid sense of personal competence in the process. Greater competence can be expected when students are intrinsically motivated and regulate and evaluate their own learning (Goldberg & Cornell, 1998).

Students want to be considered competent. It is such a compelling need that when they fail, they try to excuse themselves. They also realize that competence is what their parents and teachers desire for them. Excuses are given in an effort to prove that their failure is beyond their control, or that what is expected of them has no value and thus does not merit their conscientious efforts. Their excuse-giving is calculated to help them avoid concluding that they are incompetent when they fail after trying their best (Covington & Beery, 1976).

MOTIVATION TO LEARN

One of the critical issues in teaching is whether there is greater merit in forcing students to memorize information in which they have no interest and are unlikely to remember very long, or allowing them to select their own learning experiences with the possibility that society may consider what they have chosen to be less useful than the defined curriculum. This is usually the way the issue is presented. It carries an implicit assumption that children will inherently select topics to learn which are easily categorized as nonessential. However, this has never been conclusively confirmed.

It behooves teachers to discover the nature of the decisions students are capable of making when they are given an opportunity to help decide what they will learn and coach them regarding how to improve their selections. They should also provide students experiences designed to help prevent discipline problems in connection with participation in democratic learning communities. Experiences of this kind can help teachers recognize the degree to which students can help make valid decisions about classroom operations. Teachers have to find out if they can successfully teach children to make valid decisions about their own learning and become competent in regulating themselves.

Teachers should persist in their efforts until their students learn how to make credible decisions and become responsibly self-governing. Many students already have been conditioned by their teachers to respond disruptively in class, and it takes time to learn otherwise. Also, there is merit in allowing students to study areas of questionable content because it provides a way for teachers to capitalize on their enthusiasm. Eventually, as teachers work with them, they can help students define more appropriate subjects to study.

When educators don't believe that students can genuinely help chose their own learning activities, they attempt to create experiences that students may not find particularly interesting, but that help satisfy particular goals students may have, such as attending college or eventually being involved in a specific occupation. This is called motivation to learn. Motivation to learn should be differentiated from the usual curriculum, which emphasizes memorizing basic information. Instead students are involved in information processing, sense-making, and mastery. Teachers are careful to connect classroom learning activities to students' ultimate goals. The four following strategies are included in motivation to learn: opportunities to learn, press, support, and evaluate (Blumenfeld, Puro, & Mergendoller, 1992).

Opportunities to learn includes strategies teachers use to challenge but not overwhelm students. They also involve clarifying central ideas, presenting concrete illustrations of basic principles, relating unfamiliar information to students' personal knowledge, making explicit connections between new information and knowledge students have previously learned, posing high-level questions and probing understanding, encouraging students to summarize what they have learned, helping them to make comparisons between the various related concepts, and encouraging students to make practical applications regarding what they have learned.

With press, students are motivated to think through their responses to teacher expectations. Teachers ask students to explain and justify their responses. They also reframe questions that appear to be misunderstood and probe students when they seem to lack apprehension. In addition, teachers carefully monitor students for comprehension, rather than for just correctly answering questions, and encourage all students to participate. Finally, teachers motivate students to prepare written explanations of what they learn and create alternative representations of the information in such ways as making diagrams and charts.

Teachers use modeling and scaffolding to support student understanding. This involves modeling, thinking, and suggesting strategies for problem solving. Teachers also reduce complexity by demonstrating procedures, highlighting problems, and showing examples. In addition, they encourage students to collaborate with and acquire further insights from their peers.

In promoting evaluation, teachers emphasize understanding and learning rather than work completion, performances, comparisons between students, and right answers. They also allow students to use their mistakes to check their thinking rather than denoting their failure, and thus encourage them to take risks. When students have not performed well, they are allowed to continue working until they achieve the highest level of excellence possible.

Some of the principles associated with motivation to learn can be applied in democratic learning communities. First, teachers can share their interests with their students in areas that relate to the subjects being learned. They might share the nature of projects they are working on and show students how they have taken information they have acquired and used it to solve real problems. They can also model their personal curiosity as well as show their interest in students' questions by joining them as they work on their learning projects.

In this way, teachers can help students with low expectations of themselves by becoming more involved with them. This provides a way for teachers to offer encouragement and understand why children have experienced learning problems. As teachers work more directly with students while they are learning, they can help them make more valid assessments of their personal abilities and achievements and attain higher levels of competence.

Involvement in student learning projects also provides a way for teachers to demonstrate genuine enthusiasm in addition to highlighting their curiosity. These positive components of learning are natural outgrowths of learning communities. The teachers' curiosity becomes a model for students to imitate, but teachers can also stimulate student curiosity by asking thought-provoking questions, asking students to make predictions, or helping them to focus on what is needed for them to achieve valued objectives.

An even more effective way to stimulate students' curiosity is to have them examine interesting phenomena and ask personal questions. When questions lead to problem solving and personal research, even more interest is usually created. These interest-promoting strategies are inherent components of learning communities. In contrast, strategies commonly suggested for application in motivation to learn employ far less student autonomy and self-direction, and consequently far less interest is likely to emerge. With learning communities, teachers can also expect more student-directed discipline and far fewer classroom disruptions.

MOTIVATING STUDENTS WITH LEARNED HELPLESSNESS

Some students have low ability and in competitive school settings get further and further behind their more capable peers. Because they are behind, they are often humiliated, as their inabilities in one way or another get publicized. Eventually they even fail at tasks at which they may have been successful because they give up without trying. They spend more time trying to cover up their learning problems than actually learning.

Some students deliberately fail in school because of having low self-concepts, not because they have low ability. In reality they try to protect themselves from the conclusion that they are unable by ensuring their own failure. They deliberately fail because they are falsely certain that they cannot be successful. They try to avoid confirming their inability by orchestrating their own failure.

These children suffer from what is called learned helplessness. They have low initial expectancies for success, give up quickly when they encounter difficulty, attribute failures to lack of ability rather than to controllable causes such as insufficient effort, ascribe their success to external and uncontrollable causes like luck rather than their own abilities, and predict low success in the future (Butkowsky & Willows, 1980; Smith & Price, 1996).

It seems self-evident that students with a continuing history of failure would come to believe that they are unable to succeed. Once this belief is firmly rooted, fear of failure begins to disrupt learning and limits the students' coping abilities. Eventually, any effort to successfully learn in school is abandoned in favor of efforts to preserve self-esteem. These children require considerable effort to help them redirect their negative expectations of themselves. Three interrelated strategies can be employed to help them: attribution retraining, efficacy training, and strategy training.

Attribution retraining is designed to help students attribute failure to insufficient effort or to the use of inappropriate learning strategies rather than to lack of ability. Students are given a planned series of experiences in which they are (1) helped to set aside the potential of failure in favor of concentrating on the learning task itself, (2) assisted in analyzing their learning activities to find mistakes and to consider alternate approaches to solving problems, and (3) shown how failure is usually due to insufficient effort, lack of information, or inappropriate strategies rather than inability (Craske, 1985; Dweck & Elliott, 1983).

The key to success in attribution retraining is controlled exposure to failure. Students need to learn to cope with failure by overcoming it in the process of achieving success. Children need to see that failure comes from remediable causes. Students learn how to diagnose problems and how to correct mistakes by approaching problems in different ways. They should see that failure has no finality. It can be overturned by using new approaches. While doing this, they need to learn tolerance for frustration along with persistence in the face of difficulties and faith that continued efforts will eventually lead to success (Clifford, 1984; Rohrkemper & Corno, 1988).

In recent years more emphasis has been given in attribution retraining to helping children recognize that their failure is most likely due to ineffective strategies rather than lack of effort. This helps them realize that poor strategies may be a more cogent reason for failure, especially when they have tried their best and still fail. Insightfully, poor learning approaches have been found to be more responsible for failure than lack of effort (Brophy, 1998).

Efficacy training involves helping students set realistic goals and effectively pursue them in conjunction with believing they are achievable with reasonable effort. To accomplish this teachers (1) model how to solve problems despite apparent problems, (2) explicitly show students how to effectively accomplish learning tasks, (3) provide specific performance feedback that helps students to correct misconceptions, remedy errors, and reassure them that they are successfully learning to achieve mastery, (4) encourage students to set challenging but attainable goals, (5) help students see how their present performances surpass their prior attainments rather than how their accomplishments compare to their peers, and (6) help students realize that their success was achieved through a combination of sufficient ability and reasonable effort along with appropriate strategies (Schunk, 1985).

Strategy training involves instruction that helps students talk themselves through successful problem-solving strategies. The focus is not only on what they are doing, but also on how, when, and why it is to be done. They are taught to express their thinking verbally so that their thought processes can be more apparent not only to themselves, but to their teachers (Devine, 1987).

Students with learned helplessness need their teachers to act as resource persons rather directors and judges. Resource persons consider learning processes more important than outcomes, react to mistakes students make as natural and useful components of the learning process rather than evidence of failure, stress effort and appropriate learning strategies rather than ability and individual standards rather than group comparisons, and promote intrinsic motivation whenever it can be appropriately applied (Dweck & Elliot, 1983).

MOTIVATION IN LEARNING COMMUNITIES

It is significant that most human needs are satisfied within a social context. Human needs cannot be fulfilled without involvement with others. This helps to explain why students tend to avoid assigned schoolwork in order to socialize with their friends. Unfortunately most schools greatly limit student social interactions during learning episodes. Not only are they not encouraged, they are generally prohibited and almost never are they considered to be a strategic component of successful learning and development.

In practice, most schooling involves teacher lectures and seat work, including answering questions at the end of a chapter or filling out worksheets, rather than conducting inquiry-based investigations, engaging in simulations, participating in discussions, learning in cooperative activities, and the like (Goodlad, 1984). Also, students are independently evaluated primarily through written examinations. These activities require a relatively quiet atmosphere, with a minimum of student-to-student interaction. The result is a lot of discipline problems as students assert themselves in seeking to satisfy their needs in unacceptable ways when more legitimate means are denied them. Little wonder that talking constitutes nearly three-quarters of all classroom disruptions (Edwards, 1975).

Youth have a compelling need to interact with each other. Within a social context they are more likely to satisfy their most earnest desires. Motivation is greatly enhanced when significant learning is correlated with interpersonal interactions. Because children need frequent, meaningful interactions with each other, teachers must create many significant learning opportunities that involve social experiences. This can be meaningfully accomplished in learning communities.

In learning communities children are able to access important learning without participating in undisciplined chitchat. The need to learn and to socialize creates very motivating environment in which increased commitment can be promoted and responsible self-discipline achieved. Students find these activities motivating because community learning satisfies most all their needs in the most accommodating ways and because these kinds of experiences are authentically valued by the group. This kind of motivation is particularly potent when students are engaged in learning projects that help them to recognize and solve problems, and when these activities help them to experience a personally gratifying social life.

In order to maximize the benefit of learning communities, students should gradually assume greater responsibility for leadership. This provides added motivation. Even though students may increasingly be given greater learning autonomy, when teachers continue in a role of initiating and assessing, students easily conclude that they are not being sufficiently empowered.

In learning communities, motivation is an integral part of the experience itself. Teachers do not have to explicitly arrange learning experiences nor provide rewards. Students' own accomplishments supply the necessary motivation. In this configuration, students tend to acquire a liking for hard work because they see the positive results they can achieve when they do the best they can, particularly when they direct their own learning.

Chapter Five

Constructivist Theory, Cognitive Processing, and Learning Preferences

Because learning is the primary reason children attend school, it is imperative that it be properly understood and that learning experiences be appropriately conceptualized. Yet there are significant differences of opinion regarding the nature of learning. These disagreements are not just small discrepancies that don't matter. They constitute substantially different views that have enormous implications for the schools, not only in terms of learning but also the extent to which classroom disruptions can be prevented.

Application of natural learning processes versus contrived theories is one of the primary areas of dispute. It should be pointed out that contrived theories attempt to describe natural learning but usually incorporate a perspective that is deficient in making a sufficiently comprehensive description that takes all learning implications into account. One of the issues involves assumptions. Contrived theories usually embrace various assumptions that may or may not be true. And unfortunately, research often does not deal with validating basic assumptions, but rather focuses on practical applications. The assumptions are left untested.

One such assumption is contained in behaviorist theory, which has been heavily researched regarding its applications but not in terms of critical assumptions. For example, behaviorism assumes that humans are exclusively responders to external stimuli. No credence is given to explanations of human behavior in terms of self-guided, personal inclinations. It is assumed that all behavior can be understood as responses to external stimuli. The conclusion is to discount the usefulness and appropriateness of self-directed learning. Supposedly, everyone responds randomly unless their behavior is controlled by reinforcement or punishment.

Behaviorists believe that learning must be carefully managed by presenting carefully organized information to students, which it is assumed they simply assimilate. Students are then given feedback and rewards in order to solidify what is learned. Thus, it is believed that students do not initiate learning, but rather depend on structured learning to be imposed. It is concluded that humans have no inclination to direct their own learning.

Behaviorists believe these conceptions are necessary because we can't see inside people and determine what "makes them tick." We are thus restricted to their measurable, overt behavior. The ability to measure becomes the determinant rather than making careful observations that undoubtedly would indicate that human beings routinely engage in independent, self-directed efforts to understand and subdue their environment (Piaget, 1950). Behaviorists also conclude that classroom discipline requires systematic reinforcement and punishment. These responses to behavior are assumed to be necessary to avoid out-of-control classrooms.

CONSTRUCTIVISM

Though extensively researched, behaviorism has failed to show that all behavior is shaped by external stimuli. Yet the authenticity of behaviorism depends on this assumption being true. However, other researchers have concluded that human behavior is self-regulated. There is no question that behavior can be conditioned by rewards. This has been repeatedly demonstrated. But, this is not the sum and substance of all we do. Rather, each individual makes choices regarding whether or not to respond in one way or another when rewards are presented.

Because rewards may be desirable, we often choose to behave in ways that help us acquire them. But it is not beyond our control to refuse (Glasser, 1984). In addition, as indicated earlier, people can become conditioned to rewards. The result for many is to despise what has to be done to obtain rewards, particularly when they realize others are trying to control them. There are numerous instances where individuals have abandoned opulent lifestyles for those that are less financially rewarding in order to achieve more control over their lives. This would be unlikely if we were exclusively controlled by rewards, particularly given the fact that money is probably the most powerful reinforcer and is commonly used to satisfy many needs.

Behaviorists may claim that this is simply a matter of self-control being a more powerful reward for some people than money. However, it should be pointed out that the individual is making a choice to change rather than being managed externally. In summary, the fact that human behavior can be influenced by reinforcers and punishment doesn't mean people have no internal inclination for self-regulation. Perhaps nowhere is this more in evidence than in the public schools, where only a few high-scoring students can be enticed by grades.

Most school practices are essentially based on behavioristic principles. When students fail to measure up, more control is exercised over them. The result is lower test scores and higher dropout rates. Whenever children sense they are being controlled they tend to resist (Glasser, 1984). It should be remembered that some children readily become conditioned to grades and other incentives teachers provide. The result is for them to care less about what is learned and more for the rewards they seek and receive. Thus, they make choices that are in fact contrary to teachers' intentions as they attempt to shape children's behavior with rewards.

Nature of Constructivism

Though behaviorism continues to influence what happens in schools, the most conspicuous hope for change regarding curriculum development during the past three decades has been the constructivist theory of learning (Fensham, 1992). In general, constructivism is considered to be an extension of Piaget's work. Research has focused on understanding human cognitive processes and creating educational experiences for children that are a reflection of this reality. Constructivists are committed to teaching and learning that fits the way children actually learn (Matthews, 2000).

The basic principles of constructivism provide a stark contrast to behavioristic theory. Researchers have discovered that each individual has a unique conceptual structure of reality. This is because each person constructs a personal conception of the world based on his or her own experiences. Each person's conception is different because his or her experiences are unique. Thus, information that teachers try to transmit to students is not simply absorbed. Rather it is compared to already existing constructs and either added to them or rejected.

When a concept like the nature of an electric circuit is taught to students several times over the course of their education, it has been found that they are more likely to retain a primitive misconception that they held early in life than a more correct understanding that may have been presented in several succeeding educational experiences. Thus, students appear to resist modifying their views even when they are taught a more correct understanding of a concept. It is concluded that they are in charge of what gets included in their conceptual structure and that modifying it depends on experiences which they can accept (Osborne & Wittrock, 1983). Changes are more likely when students are involved in discovering new information rather than simply having it presented to them.

Constructivism is a theory about the parameters of human knowledge. It concludes that all knowledge is a product of each individual's own thinking. A person is unable to have any direct or unmediated understanding of external or objective reality. Rather, each person must construct his or her own understanding through personal experience. Consequently, the nature of learning is profoundly influenced by an individual's experiences and the way each person has of viewing and processing information acquired in these activities (Confrey, 1990; Fosnot, 1996). The result is for the conceptual organization of any person to be unique to him or her and significantly different from that held by anyone else.

This is a particularly significant finding for teachers. Their ordinary mode of teaching incorrectly assumes that children absorb information as it is presented. Because teachers usually provide all their students the same learning experiences, it is tacitly assumed that their students hold similar views of what is transmitted to them, and that they do not have any problem simply adding what is presented to their current understanding, automatically making corrections as appropriate. Teachers presume that they can induce children to change misconceptions by simply giving them new, more correct knowledge on the subject.

Evidence indicates this doesn't happen as teachers hope. It has been found that even college students have often retained misconceptions acquired as small children even though they have subsequently received correct information on the subject several times (Osborne & Wittrock, 1983).

Because the brain does not passively absorb information, but rather actively constructs its own interpretations of what is learned and idiosyncratically draws inferences from it, teachers tend to draw incorrect conclusions when their students appear not to have learned what they teach. They may conclude that students are not motivated or that they are slow learners rather than correctly recognizing that they simply have not internalized what has been taught in the form in which it was presented. In fact students may have simply retained old conceptions and rejected the new information presented to them.

It is important for teachers to recognize that the brain selectively ignores some information and attends to other information. Some concepts are incorporated into current knowledge structures while others are not. To learn with understanding, learners must actively construct meaning. That is simply how the brain operates (Phillips, 2000). Nothing just gets absorbed as it is presented. For true comprehension to take place, the individual must invent a model or explanation for it that organizes the information to fit their logic, real-world experiences, or both.

Students retrieve information from long-term memory and use their information-processing strategies to generate meaning from incoming information or to organize it, code it, and store it in long-term memory. Often new information is simply discarded because it does not seem relevant to the individual. Changing current conceptions is more likely to occur when the individual engages in personal inquiries and personally discovers information that can justifiably be used to make appropriate adjustments. In addition, teachers cannot understand the cognitive structures and functions of their students without observing them interacting with others in a social-intellectual context and within a culture (Fosnot, 1996).

Some theorists believe that the reality people construct of the world is limited to sensory inputs. From this point of view, information must be perceived and stored as pictorial images. However, people do not create meaning from sensory inputs. Instead, sensory inputs must first be converted into concepts like pressure, elasticity, force, and stress. Each of these ideas has to be defined in order to have meaning. Otherwise, they cannot be cognitively related to other information and structures of knowledge individuals have created.

Also, it is important for teachers to realize that these definitions are not simply understood from direct experience. Experts in various fields have defined them and thus students can't simply ascertain them on their own. These definitions are within the public domain of knowing and are not simply personal. Thus, learning cannot be thought of as 100 percent personal even though one's conceptualization of what is taught is personal. Consequently one's understanding of conceptual knowledge may in part be framed by others, but what ends up in the human brain is strictly determined by the individual.

Constructivism and Instruction

Since knowledge is personally constructed instead of simply being transmitted by teachers and absorbed by students, how can the complex conceptual schemes be acquired that have taken the best minds hundreds of years to build up? Obviously students can't be expected, through their own direct investigations, to gain an understanding of what has been painstakingly learned by scholars. For example, what is the likelihood that children on their own would think to address concepts like genes, democracy, velocity, acceleration, gravity, and the like? And even if they inadvertently happened onto such concepts, what would be the nature of their understanding? Also, it is unlikely that schools are able to provide students with meaningful, direct experiences with phenomena that require sophisticated equipment to study.

The question is how can students come to know information that is in large part abstract and consequently removed from their experience, that has no connection to their prior conceptions, and that is alien to common sense and in conflict with everyday experience, expectations, and concepts (Matthews, 2000)? If students are to have access to the knowledge of the world, they must go beyond their own inexperienced inquiry efforts. They need to have access to bonafide systems of knowledge which they can personally explore. They also need to see models as well as conventional knowledge of the subjects being studied (Solomon, 1994).

In this process, teachers must not ignore the fact that knowledge construction is essentially a personal thing. The challenge is to provide students opportunities to investigate knowledge of the various subjects along with doing their own research. As part of their efforts to conduct personal investigations they should examine what has been done by scholars so that they can properly relate it to their own research. When this is consistently done, students are more inclined to visualize their own conceptions within the context of the knowledge base that has been created by scholars. When students become well acquainted with the knowledge base, their research has meaning as well as an appropriate intellectual context. As they attempt to integrate conventional knowledge with their own research efforts, they acquire more correct conceptions.

Teachers should be wary of simply explaining concepts to students, illustrating them, or even attempting to show the interconnections between areas of information. Explicitly teaching information in this way is inconsistent with the way humans learn. We are not able to abandon natural learning practices just to fit a particular teaching method. This is one of the dilemmas of constructivist theory. The teaching practices that are almost universally used do not fit the way we learn, and students resist modifying their natural inclinations.

Interestingly, it is not clear whether this is exclusively a matter of inability or if it is also a matter of choice. Some researchers believe we are hardwired to learn according to constructivist theory, but it very well may be that we resist on the grounds of preferring self-direction. What we do know is that with traditional instruction, students may incorrectly construct meaning and resist efforts to modify their thinking (Osborne & Wittrock, 1983).

It should be noted that if students resist altering their views, an entirely different problem is created than if they simply find difficulty processing information transmitted to them by traditional means. Discipline problems can more readily be attributed to incompatibility between teaching and learning than students' supposed negative natural inclinations.

Osborne and Wittrock (1983) provide critical information about student characteristics as they learn. This research was done in science but applies to other subjects as well. They find that:

- Children understand the world around them from their own point of view.
- The understanding of the world held by older students is essentially the same as that which they had as young children even though they have experienced considerable additional instruction on these subjects.

- Children's initial ideas of phenomena are amazingly tenacious and resistant to change.
- When children's ideas are changed through instruction, the changes are commonly quite different from those the teacher intended.
- Students consider each lesson in the classroom to be an isolated event, while their teachers assume that students appreciate the connecting links between lessons.
- Student purposes in connection with a particular lesson are often subtly but significantly different from those intended by the teacher.
- Students often show little interest in those features of instruction that the teacher or textbook writers consider critical.
- Pupils' organization of knowledge is frequently not the same as that which teachers assume they have.
- Children unknowingly modify the information presented by their teachers so it is not in conflict with their earlier conceptions.

These data suggest that teachers should be observant so they can ascertain learning problems during instruction. Obviously they can't take for granted that students will assimilate the knowledge they are transmitting. It is essential that student thinking should be taken into account and their current conceptual structures considered in the instructional process. Students need to confront inconsistencies in their thinking, but the way in which this is done must involve student exploration along with properly configured conceptual arrangements.

To reiterate, simply presenting information to students is unlikely to help. Instead, teachers need to interact with their students and help them mount a search for understanding that promotes inquiry and investigation. By involving students in helping to create conceptual structures there is greater assurance that they will eventually obtain a correct understanding of the various subjects.

Students need the assistance of their teachers in order to achieve an accurate understanding of what they are trying to learn. From the constructivist point of view, teachers need to help them make connections between new information and conceptual networks they already have. In order for knowledge to become useful in a generative sense—usable for interpreting new situations, solving problems, and thinking and reasoning—students have to learn how to frame and elaborate critical questions about what is being taught and learn how to examine new information in relation to more familiar understandings.

In this process, they build new conceptual structures that are more sophisticated and useful in dealing with problems they confront. Otherwise the new information remains inaccessible and cannot be understood and used for solving problems in everyday life (Resnick & Klopfer, 1989). This, of course, is the ordinary consequence of traditional school instruction. Most of what is taught remains unusable because students have not accentuated their understanding by incorporating the new information into their existing knowledge structures.

Knowledge construction is much more effective and efficient when students are helped by their teachers to relate new information to their existing background knowledge (Adams, 1990). As already mentioned, to enhance student understanding teachers must be careful not to assume all students come with the same conceptual knowledge. Each obviously has had different experiences and each has idiosyncratically constructed their own view of the world. What is needed are instructional strategies that allow students some degree of independent judgment and self-direction while at the same time helping them incorporate a broad base of knowledge into their personal conceptions.

Learning communities are particularly adept at providing this kind of experience. In addition, teaching and learning must proceed from concrete to abstract. Nothing is understood initially as an abstraction. Instead it is understood within a concrete context, which is supplied by previous experiences and existing knowledge (Anderson, 1984). For example, suppose most students in a class are ready to learn about multiple causation.The teachers may choose to help them develop this capacity by examining the reasons commonly given regarding U.S. involvement in the war in Iraq.

Various possible scenarios could be researched by students. They might discover some of the following suggested reasons for the United States going to war: (1) the necessity of unseating Saddam Hussein because he supposedly supported global terrorism, (2) the CIA report of the presence in Iraq of weapons of mass destruction, (3) the fact that a prominent former Iraqi government official indicated that Saddam Hussein had ties to terrorist organizations, (4) the fact that Saddam Hussein had already used weapons of mass destruction in the form of chemicals to kill many Iraqi citizens, particularly among the Kurdish population, (5) the fact that earlier Iraqi forces had invaded Kuwait, which threatened to destabilize the entire region, (6) the threat still existed that Iraq might invade other countries due to its continued building of military strength, and (7) the possibility that allowing Saddam Hussein's government to continue would be a threat to the world's oil supply on which the United States is increasingly dependent.

Once a set of possible scenarios has been determined, additional research may be conducted to elaborate an understanding of each possibility. After this, class discussions would be held with an effort made to determine the relative importance of each suggested reason for U.S. involvement. This way students can be led to understand the tendency for conclusions to be drawn in terms of single causation rather than recognizing the possibility for multiple causes. Finally, students would be asked to consider multiple causes and the relative importance of each factor and to create a conceptual structure which may show interrelationships and relative strengths of all factors.

In this learning strategy, students are able to expand their list of causes. They likely will already have heard single causes expounded. Finding several more possibilities, along with visualizing multiple causes, promotes intellectual growth, helping students develop the capacity for abstract thought. This is one of the most critical skills they can develop as part of their education. In this exercise, not only do students learn how to more effectively process complex information, they are also helped to obtain more comprehensive views of world events of which they may have had too limited an understanding.

When children's current views of various phenomena are inaccurate or unsuitable for the concepts being learned, using them will interfere with learning (Alvermann, Smith, & Readence, 1985). Commonly these inaccurate schemas are part of the primitive view children have of the world, which is based on their naive experiences. For example, small children while riding in a car at night believe the moon is following them because it appears to be moving relative to them. They also have the age-old view that the sun revolves around the earth, for that is the way it appears until they are helped to realize that it is the earth's rotation that explains what they observe.

As already mentioned, children develop these views from their own observations and, once established, are difficult to modify. Children ordinarily hold on to their misconceptions tenaciously. Simply explaining the correct interpretation of these phenomena won't cause a change in their views. Instead it is far more effective to have them perform investigations so that by their own initiative, information is gathered with which to modify misconceptions.

From the constructivist point of view, teachers must allow their students to raise their own questions, generate their own hypotheses and models of possibilities, and test them to determine their validity. Sometimes this can be done through examining various phenomena themselves. Other times assessing the research of various experts is necessary. Children need to confront contradictions and attempt to determine what the contradicting elements are.

Teachers must realize that reflective abstraction is the driving force of learning. In an effort to acquire meaning humans inherently seek to organize and generalize across their experiences. Students should thus have opportunities to make connections between various experiences and seek to abstractly construct meaning. This can best be accomplished through dialogue within learning communities.

In this context, learners are responsible for defending, proving, justifying, and communicating their ideas to classmates. The "big ideas" that eventually emerge are learner-constructed even though they may in part be based on the knowledge obtained from experts. These constructs can be used to generalize across experiences and often require the undoing or reorganizing of earlier conceptions. This process can be expected to continue throughout the entire schooling experience (Fosnot, 1996).

Constructivism in Learning Communities

Learning communities are particularly useful in helping students reconstruct erroneous conceptions. In this learning configuration, they not only investigate various phenomena in which they are interested, but they are also involved with others in discussions. In these interactions, they are exposed to input from their peers, which helps them become aware of previously unknown information with which to expand their cognitive structures.

When they are exposed to ideas that are contrary to their own, they are more likely to carefully examine their own understanding and beliefs and become more willing to reconstruct them. These interactions should consist of sustained dialogues and discussions in which students pursue topics in depth. This provides them with information that is cogent enough for them to interact at higher cognitive levels and acquire a more meaningful view of the world along with critical implications and ramifications (Pearson & Iran-Negate, 1998).

Participating in learning communities not only provides students an effective way to learn conceptual knowledge and reconstruct their misconceptions, but they also learn viable life skills that are unavailable to them in traditional schooling. This is because their social interactions are not of the frivolous kind engaged in primarily outside of class, but rather are employed within the context of learning. Many times their learning agenda may have critical social components. They may, for example, undertake studies of social phenomena that relate to personal relationships. They also routinely engage in an ethic of care, which helps in the development of important skills that they will apply throughout their lives as they meet and interact with others in various social environments.

It is wise for learning communities to become involved in communities at large in order to supply students with a more authentic learning environment. Sometimes outside community members can become involved with students in their research. Other times they supply opportunities for students to have apprenticeship experiences. It should be noted that the knowledge and skills provided in schools have been abstracted and removed from the settings where they originated. Thus, schools artificially separate knowing from doing and in the process reduce the effectiveness of learning. As a result, students fail to learn how to make applications of what they acquire in school to real-life situations.

It is unfortunate for children educated in traditional schools that their cognitive development comes from abstract conceptualizations outlined in textbooks rather than arising from real-life situations with the natural settings, purposes, and tasks from which they were originally created. If students are to retain useful knowledge, they need to acquire it in natural settings, using the methods for learning that are more suited to that setting.

It is difficult for children to ascertain authentic meanings outside real contexts. It is significant that their own early learning experiences took place almost entirely within real-life contexts, which had the potential for clearer understanding and provided the means with which to make applications of what was learned. Ordinarily their learning was self-directed toward solving problems or simply acquiring an understanding of the world around them.

One of the reasons many children flounder in school is because there they are subjected to learning experiences without a context as they try to absorb information for which they see no connection to real life. It is alien to their natural learning disposition and this in all likelihood is why they struggle to remember what they are taught. Their inclination is to restrict their learning to those things they see as instrumental in fulfilling their needs. Without this personal connection, they don't clearly see the usefulness of what is presented to them in the classroom.

Therefore, their reason for learning becomes one of satisfying their parents and teachers, getting good grades and achieving recognition, or qualifying for college admission or a profession. These objectives may have merit, but they are not consistent with the way children naturally process information. In addition, curiosity also drives children's learning. Unfortunately, most teachers see children's curiosity as a nemesis to their teaching desires. Obviously, curiosity leads children down significantly different learning pathways and frustrates the structure most teachers consider essential. Thus, a very natural, effective way to drive learning is thwarted, leaving teachers with the necessity of filling in with other motivating strategies, which are far less effective and often create problems.

THE THINKING PROCESS

Constructivism describes a realistic, natural process of learning and suggests a departure from traditional conceptions. It represents a way to provide students a more viable education, one in which they can become more autonomously responsible, as well as helping them to achieve their true intellectual potential. Additional insights regarding how the brain operates are available through the study of hemisphericity and multiple intelligences as well as through an analysis of the thinking process.

Hemisphericity

It is essential that teaching and learning be geared to the way in which thinking naturally occurs. Critical insights were obtained regarding this process in the 1960s when Robert Sperry, a psychologist and neurobiologist, made some startling discoveries regarding the human brain that earlier were essentially unknown. In an effort to prevent seizures in an epilepsy patient, he separated the two hemispheres of the brain at the corpus callosum. In the process he discovered that each of the hemispheres had separate modes of functioning and processed incoming stimuli from the environment in different and often contradictory ways. Each hemisphere had its own private sensations, perceptions, thoughts, and ideas (Sperry, 1975).

It was also learned that even with the intact brain, each hemisphere makes its own unique perceptions of the world, stores this perceived memory, and then shares it with the other hemisphere. However, each hemisphere performs entirely different mental operations on stimuli received (Gazzaniga, 1968). Yet, even though each hemisphere has its own sphere of operations, it influences the other hemisphere when the connection between them remains intact. Each hemisphere perceives on its own and engages in its own patterns of thought, but each influences the other by inhibiting or facilitating particular features to keep the effect harmonious and consistent. The left hemisphere tends to be the more dominant (Sperry, 1974).

Brain Processing and Hemisphericity

Each hemisphere specializes in quite different processes. The left hemisphere is skilled at a rapid understanding and retention of verbally expressed ideas, while the right hemisphere is involved in processing images and engaging in spacial tasks (Milner, 1969; Ornstein, 1978). Because each hemisphere has a different system for processing data, disparate results are arrived at despite receiving the same data (Bogen, 1968).

Even though the hemispheres perform different functions, any particular person tends to favor one hemisphere over the other and process data in this hemisphere regardless of the nature of the task to be performed (Ornstein, 1978). Thus, students do not differentiate learning tasks in terms of brain function, but rather routinely process data in the preferred hemisphere even though the success of using that particular hemisphere for that specific task may be limited. This helps explain why students experience difficulty in performing certain tasks assigned in their classes and why students become frustrated and even panic when required to engage in certain kinds of learning activities. This of course leads to classroom discipline problems.

Left-hemisphere learners prefer using technical, scientific, rational, analytical, logical, factual, convergent, and quantitative skills. These individuals learn well from lectures, skillfully read, and excel in test taking. In contrast, right-hemisphere learners are more visual and holistic. They are imaginative and divergent in their thinking, more adept at hands-on activities, and more able to engage in holistic conceptualizations. Very few people have the use of both hemispheres in a nondominant manner, although it is an advantage to those having both abilities (Smith, 1992).

Restricting learning activities to a single hemisphere unnecessarily handicaps some students even though this is a common practice. Traditional schools emphasize the left hemisphere almost entirely. This is particularly true in subjects like English, math, history, and science. Yet most teachers fail to recognize the negative implications of limiting learning activities to a single hemisphere.

It is estimated that about 80 percent of the general population primarily operates out of the left hemisphere. This is convenient because much of the work assigned in school is best performed out of that hemisphere. But, of course, that leaves the other 20 percent having to perform left-hemisphere mental operations using the right hemisphere. Obviously they experience trouble. This is evident in a study by Piatt (1979) wherein it was found that only 12 percent of the boys and 26 percent of the girls in an alternative high school for dropouts were left-brain dominant. As might be expected, students with right-brain dominance found it necessary to leave traditional schools in greater numbers and become involved in programs more conductive to their thinking mode.

The fact that left-brained students greatly outnumber their right-brained counterparts may not necessarily be a genetic problem but rather an environmental one. This is because it appears that there is an increase in left-brain functioning among children over time. In fact, most children are born right-hemisphere dominant, but some time later the majority primarily use the left brain. It has been suggested that this is so because school is so left-hemisphere oriented that it promotes more left-brain functioning. Yet a significant number of children continue right-brain functioning even though a great number of them make a transition.

Interestingly, the question has been raised regarding whether or not this is the kind of effect that is most desirable, or if more right-brain functioning would be worthwhile in society and should be supported. It consequently has been recommended that children be given more experiences to assist them in developing visualization, imagination, and sensory/perceptual abilities (Rennels, 1967). Piatt (1979) suggests that a full life for many goes begging because of abandonment of right-brain functioning with its richness.

Sex Differences and Hemisphericity

As schools are presently configured, girls have more success than boys because they operate more out of the left hemisphere, while boys are more
right-hemisphere oriented. This shows up particularly in girls' more advanced vocabulary development. Language functions are more compartmen-
talized in male brains and more globally distributed in female brains. Thus,
females use both hemispheres for language, while males use only the left.
Males who are right-hemisphere dominant have an even greater disadvantage
trying to compete verbally with girls. These differences are genetically pro-
grammed and not mediated by hormonal differences (Sax, 2005).

Girls are also more adept at auditory learning. As newborns they hear
much better than boys and the advantage gets bigger over time (Corso,
2005). The result is for girls to be more easily distracted by noise, thus
making it difficult for them to learn in noisy classrooms. Girls can be distracted by noise levels that are 10 times softer than noise levels that distract
boys (Elliot, 1971).

Boys favor visual and tactile learning. They tend to want to touch everything in the classroom and are much more oriented toward gross motor
movement than girls. Consequently, they are far more likely to annoy their
teachers through their movements. This is probably the reason boys are more
frequently diagnosed with attention deficit hyperactivity disorder (ADHD).
They are naturally more physically active than girls, and teachers consequently have more trouble managing them (James, 2007).

Accordingly, there is a growing belief that behavior once diagnosed as
ADHD may actually be the result of restrictive classroom practices rather
than other causes. It is important to note that some of the boys who are
diagnosed with ADHD are unusually gifted and creative. Their curious natures, which are intrinsic to children, do not articulate well with usual classroom routines (Hartnett, Nelson, & Rinn, 2004).

Boys and girls are also different in terms of color preferences. Girls like
red, orange, green, and beige. Boys prefer black, gray, silver, and blue. This
is an important distinction to make because female teachers predominate in
elementary school—95 percent in kindergarten. It is common for female
teachers to encourage boys in their classes to add "more color" to their
artwork, thus unwittingly imposing their own biases on boys (Sax, 2005).

Boys and girls also process emotions differently. This is because girls use
the cerebral cortex while boys use the amygdala. The result is for girls to
want to talk about their emotions while boys do not. Asking boys to talk
about their emotions creates an expectation for them to use connections
between two parts of the brain that normally don't interact. Also, boys are
much more likely to engage in risky behavior. They get a pleasant tingle by
exposing themselves to danger. Their amygdala reacts to dangerous situa-

tions by stimulating the endocrine system to excrete the appropriate hormones to raise the heart rate and blood pressure and prepare the muscles for activity. The result is for boys to consistently overestimate their own ability, while girls underestimate their abilities when facing risky situations.

When children are shielded from possible injury, it makes them more risk aversive. In order to build character and provide children with self-confidence, resilience, and self-reliance, it is wise to allow them to experience a few scrapes and cuts. Girls in particular need training in taking risks in order to help them avoid experiencing excessive failure (Mogel, 2001). Otherwise they will generalize their failures as they interpret them as having disappointed adults. Rather than generalizing their failures, boys are more inclined to see them as relevant to specific events. This is probably due to their relative lack of concern with pleasing adults (Pomerantz, Altermatt, & Saxton, 2002).

Boys and girls react differently to stress. Girls experience a nauseated feeling under stress that emanates from the parasympathetic nervous system. Boys on the other hand process stress in the sympathetic nervous system and instead experience a thrill (Sax, 2005). They seem unable to think through the consequences of their actions (Nagel, 2005). The decline of serotonin levels during adolescence predisposes them to impulsivity, risky behavior, anger, hostility, and suicidal tendencies (Bradley, 2003).

Early exposure to stress or violence causes the brain to reorganize itself, increasing receptor sites for alertness chemicals. This increases reactivity and blood pressure, making the child more impulsive and aggressive in school (Kotulak, 1996). Most emotional intelligence is learned in children's first year. This includes disappointment, pleasure, anxiety, sadness, fearfulness, pride, and feeling ashamed, delighted or apologetic (Wilson, Willner, Kurtz, & Nadel, 1986). If children's emotions are not properly attuned during their first year they ordinarily end up being emotionally corrupt (Thal, Tobias, & Morrison, 1991).

Parents act as templates for their children. Even their gestures are important. Thus, parents can communicate fearfulness by placing limitations on children, even with facial expressions, in situations like when they are learning to walk or crawl (Kagan, 1994). It is interesting to note that the human brain releases the neurotransmitters of pleasure in response to feeling cared for and valued.

Involvement in challenging problem-solving situations also has positive effects on brain function. As children feel more capable of solving problems, their feelings of competence increase. When this happens fewer catacholomines are released, which is the body's natural response to stress. In problem solving, it doesn't matter whether or not the problem being worked on is solved. Engaging in the process is sufficient to have a positive effect (Healy, 1990).

Hemisphericity and Brain Functions

Several neurotransmitters are involved in natural, intrinsic motivation. For mild cognitive motivation the individual experiences an increased level of norepinephrine or dopamine. With more active motivation, the levels of peptide vasopressin or adrenaline increase. All of these motivating chemicals are encouraged by eliminating threat and allowing children to set their own goals and become involved in teamwork where they receive success and positive social affirmation. Teachers who emphasize lecture and fact accumulation consequently violate an important brain growth principle.

Essentially, humans are social beings and their brains grow in a social environment. Because conceptual meanings are forged through social interaction, many classrooms fail to provide the growth experiences student interactions would produce. Talking, sharing, and discussing are critical because we are biologically wired to communicate with each other. In addition, emotions are essential in helping the mind to focus. They also help the individual make decisions faster and of higher quality.

Nearly everything we experience has an emotional tone to it. Emotions help stimulate a more activated and chemically stimulated brain, which help the individual recall things better. When emotions are suppressed, depressed cognitive functioning and discipline problems are often the result (Healy, 1990). Brain systems are so interconnected that the chemicals of emotion are released virtually simultaneously with cognition. This link between feelings and meaning is processed at an unconscious level in the middle of the brain and brain stem area (Hobson, 1994; LeDoux, 1996).

Humans naturally search for meaning in order to understand their world and use it to satisfy their curiosity and needs. Children, who because of their excessively structured school experiences become compliant and consequently good "technicians," often experience failure when demands for comprehension increase later in their schooling. Due to the lack of emotional content they experience and the resultant reduction in associated brain stimulation, they simply can't assemble complex conceptional information and make sense out of it (Healy, 1994).

Because girls are more adept at what schooling calls for, it is often assumed that they develop faster than boys. Rather, the various regions of the brain develop in a different sequence in boys as compared to girls. The area of the brain that involves language and fine motor skills matures in girls about six years earlier than in boys. However, the areas of the brain responsible for targeting and spatial memory mature about four years earlier in boys. All in all, this puts boys at a disadvantage in the early years of school. This has been an increasing problem due to the move to make kindergarten more academically oriented rather than developmentally appropriate.

One of the most glaringly inappropriate tactics is to indiscriminately try to teach children to read at a particular grade level, and when they fail to label them as handicapped, when in fact brain functioning is the factor most likely responsible. This stigmatizing approach can have long-lasting negative effects that are difficult to overcome. The result is an alarming increase in the use of drugs like Ritalin and Adderall to treat ADHD and medications like Prozac, Zoloft, Paxil, Celea, Lexapro, Wellbutrin, Pamerlor, and Elavil to treat depression (Zito, et al., 2003).

School appears to be customized in favor of girls. Thus, 80 percent of the books selected in elementary schools cater to girls' desires. This, along with the various attributes of boys that are incompatible with school operations, encourages problems, which then are treated with drugs. Educators not only need to recognize the cause of the problems children suffer in school, they also need to provide children experiences that are more compatible with their basic natures, inclinations, and development.

Multiple Intelligences

Surprisingly, children are able to master many skills during the first years of life with very little instruction. They quickly become proficient in speaking their native language, as well as in a good number of physical skills like throwing balls, riding bicycles, and dancing. Ironically, even very young children are able to learn complex symbol systems like language, as well as art forms like music and drawing and personal theories regarding how the world operates, and yet many experience difficulty with what is taught in their school classrooms. This is due to the fact that children possess different minds and therefore learn, remember, perform, and understand in significantly different ways (Gardner, 1991).

Gardner identifies eight distinct ways children have of knowing and representing the world, with each having its own unique rules, codes, and symbols. Students operate from different intellectual perspectives and consequently have different approaches to problems and learn in different ways. Each learner has a unique mix of these intelligences, with varying tendencies toward a predominant learning orientation. This creates problems for children who have intellectual capabilities that are inconsistent with school expectations. The intelligences identified by Gardner include bodily-kinesthetic, linguistic, logical-mathematical, visual-spatial, musical, interpersonal, intrapersonal, and naturalistic.

In most classes bodily-kinesthetically oriented students find very few opportunities to learn effectively. This is particularly so in the academic subjects like math, science, English, and social studies. They are better suited to activities like drama, role-playing, simulations, dancing, games, demonstrations, sports, and field trips. To the extent teachers can incorporate such activities into academically oriented classes, they should. For example, a teacher might have students participate in a creative drama regarding an issue in science like evolution. Basic science concepts could be incorporated into such a production.

Linguistically oriented students excel at understanding meaning through language. They are particularly adept at writing stories and poems. This learning inclination is especially useful for students who wish to compare their ideas with classmates. Because so much school learning is linguistically symbolic and inaccessible to students with other learning orientations, it is wise to have linguistically oriented children help their classmates in such configurations as learning communities.

Logical-mathematically oriented students are highly organized, logical, and well equipped to use rule-based systems to create and understand meaning. Children with this orientation can help their peers identify problems to research, help organize research strategies, and provide insights in drawing appropriate conclusions from data they collect. Teachers who want to promote this kind of thinking can (1) use diverse questioning strategies, (2) pose open-ended problems for students to examine and solve, (3) provide the means for students to construct models of key concepts, (4) ask students to predict and verify logical outcomes in their research, (5) provide a means for students to discern patterns and connections between diverse phenomena, (6) ask students to elaborate and justify their statements and opinions, and (7) provide students with a plethora of things to observe and investigate.

Visual-spatial intelligence involves creating and comprehending meaning through visual and spatial symbols and conceptions. Most school subjects contain possibilities for promoting visual-spatial learning. For example, students may create flow charts that represent complex processes, concept maps that show relationships between ideas, models of various structures and processes, and visual representations of stories or poems that students are writing. Thus, in biology, students might be asked to construct a cell model with all its organelles arranged in their proper configuration. In language arts, students might create puppets or paint murals and backdrops, as well as illustrate literature by creating storyboards. To do this, students need to be supplied with appropriate tools and materials.

Children with a musical orientation are particularly skilled at composing and performing various kinds of music. Because music is ordinarily thought of as exclusively belonging to the extra-curricular program, teachers in academic areas need to come up with inventive ways to promote this learning inclination in their classrooms. For example, music can be studied scientifically in science classrooms. Also, some kinds of music are known to accentuate learning. It can also help promote zest and warmth and create a variety of emotions and images. Teachers may want to have their students create music for special purposes, such as composing a class song.

Children with interpersonal skill have an unusual ability to understand society and help work through social problems and processes well. They are particularly proficient in helping others avoid conflict and in successfully dealing with conflict when it occurs. They tend to be more sensitive regarding the needs of others and are adept at helping all members of the class to participate. They are also effective in promoting helpful communications, incorporating values and priorities in group deliberations, clarifying perceptions of others regarding confusing situations, and helping classmates understand that the learning approaches and personalities of members of the learning community can be different and have enhancing or denigrating effects on group members.

These youngsters are proficient in helping learning communities function properly while assisting classmates to gain the maximum benefit from their participation. Teachers can promote the development of this attribute by helping students appreciate divergent opinions and working with others who have different points of view. This is best accomplished when groups are actually composed of members representing different races, classes, and cultures.

Intrapersonal intelligence involves self-reflection philosophically, psychologically, and religiously. These individuals employ higher-order thinking in developing a system of values. They are particularly adept at creating consistent value systems along with understanding related emotions and feelings. These students understand the necessity of their personal preferences and values being consistent with social expectations and standards. They tend to be socially well adjusted and have an adequate understanding of themselves and appropriate modes of expression. They have an ability to see how their values articulate with important societal morals and ideas.

Self-reflection can be enhanced through journal writing. Teachers can help their students develop intrapersonal skill by encouraging them to write about their self-explorations, investigate their personal philosophies while examining how these articulate with social values, and determine what they have learned from life experiences and how these experiences have shaped their values and life objectives. Children can write about personal weaknesses and strengths along with engaging in self-improvement activities. This way they are able to achieve greater personal understanding and consequently make enhancing life adjustments.

Children with naturalistic intelligence use the natural world to create and understand meaning. They do this by observing, reflecting, making connections, classifying, integrating, and communicating their perceptions of the natural and man-made worlds. As they visualize patterns and relationships between living organisms and various physical entities, they are able to make meaningful distinctions in the natural world. This can be cultivated by encouraging students to make astute observations, conduct research, and devise

explanations regarding their interpretations and conclusions. Study orientations might include such things as change, adaption, balance, biotic resources, diversity, competition, cycles, patterns, and populations (Carreiro,
1998; Gardner, 1994).

There is a dearth of opportunities in school for children to develop various intellectual capacities, or for children who already have these orientations to magnify them. In schools where memorizing information is emphasized, none of the orientations is properly promoted. Schools that focus on
conceptual understanding encourage linguistic and logical-mathematical development to some degree, but the other skills are almost completely absent
except in some extra-curricular activities or special classes like art and music.

Some students may excel in art and music but fail to be successful in their
other classes. Students with logical-mathematical or linguistic orientations
may never really understand and appreciate music and art and be inept in
comprehending themselves and society. In highly structured schools there
are hardly any opportunities to develop intrapersonal capabilities.

Not only teachers, but also administrators, parents, and other interested
parties are unlikely to consider all the intelligences to be legitimate for inclusion in school curricula. In taking this position, they are in effect saying that
some children have no legitimacy in school. This represents the ultimate in
human ignorance and intolerance. It is like saying that what many of these
children represent is of no value to society. It is assumed that with such
intellectual inclinations they cannot meet life expectancies. In essence, these
children are by definition unfit for acceptable roles in society. Children who
lack these so-called respectable skills are simply judged to be inferior to,
rather than different from, their peers.

Actually society needs people in all the categories of intelligence. Only
by involving everyone can valid insights be gained about how to function in
a complex society. Learning communities are also benefitted by having students of all kinds engaging in a wide variety of learning activities while
accentuating all the intelligences. Children who are involved in such a learning configuration gain a necessary understanding of the real world that sur-
rounds them and an ability to successfully function there.

All children have a different combination of intellectual abilities and
commonly favor a limited number of them. It would be well for teachers to
promote the development of all capacities in all children. This greatly broad-
ens each student's capability to function successfully in society. It seems
wise for teachers to provide students opportunities to achieve in the areas in
which they excel while at the same time developing skills in other areas. This
allows all children to gain greater skill and needed recognition in the areas of
greatest interest while accentuating their skills in other domains. This, no

doubt, would involve learning experiences that differ substantially from the ordinary.

There needs to be a wider range of valued learning experiences. None should be relegated to a lesser status. Thus, children who have intellectual capabilities that have been historically ignored in school can be provided a way of seeing that what they prefer doing is important. Many topics of worth can be approached in at least eight different ways that to some degree map onto multiple intelligences. In doing this, teachers need to abandon the common, misguided effort to cover everything, planned in advance. Fuller understanding is far more likely to be achieved if students encounter learning episodes in a variety of guises and contexts and if adjustments are made as instruction proceeds.

The best way to bring this about is to draw on all the intelligences that are relevant to a particular topic in as many legitimate ways as possible and abandon preset conceptual structures that are the same for everyone. Most schools throughout history have been uniform in teaching the same things in the same way while assessing student achievement in a similar manner. This is believed to be fair. However, it is fundamentally unfair because it privileges those who have strong linguistic and logical-mathematical intelligences, making school difficult for those who have different intellectual profiles (Gardner, 2006).

The Frank Smith Model of Thinking

Thinking is not exclusively intellectual. Actually, the way a person thinks may be determined extensively by emotional or personality considerations rather than by intellectual ability. Thinking is often characterized by such terms as *analyze, categorize, classify, conceptualize, conjecture, create, deliberate, discover, explain, examine, hypothesize, imagine, infer, invent, judge, meditate, organize, postulate, predict, reason, reflect, speculate,* and *theorize,* just to mention a few. However, these terms refer to things people do, not to the activities in their brains. There is no evidence that these terms describe different brain functions.

The brain is often likened to a computer in terms of being able to manipulate, store, and retrieve information. But it can do a whole lot more. For example, it is able to create personal realities, both actual and imaginary. It can examine alternatives, create narratives, and relate personal experiences to all its functions. Intriguingly, in the process of exploring the world and trying to make sense out of it, the brain picks up an enormous amount of information incidentally without the individual willing it. It is able to think about what the current world is like, what it might be in the future, and even about unknown imaginary worlds.

Thus, the brain can determine the present in connection with the past, along with conceptions of the future. Without this capacity, the world would be incomprehensible. It is important to realize that thinking is driven by feelings that help us avoid bewilderment, achieve satisfaction, escape frustration, and confront our personal identity as both the originator and main actor in the ongoing saga of our lives.

It is curious that thinking occurs when we aren't cognizant of it. Thus, we can walk down the street avoiding collisions with other pedestrians while thinking of a wide variety of things, but nothing in particular. Unawareness regarding what we are thinking doesn't signify its absence. Despite the absence of conscious effort and the ease with which we think, it is actually quite complex. Consequently, even while thinking casually, our brains routinely take many considerations into account, including balancing contrary plans, purposes, and intentions while helping us incorporate a smooth flow to daily life. People rarely behave as they do for a single reason. The brain skillfully analyzes alternatives and multiple purposes in the course of deciding on a particular action.

Even though we often think of what we sense through our eyes as pictures, they are not. Rather, the neural impulses received by the brain are interpreted and integrated into already existing images. This can be confusing, for the brain must decide what is producing the neural impulses, and from this create sights, sounds, and other perceptions received. Though the brain can be mistaken about the perceptual images received, it is amazingly accurate. It is all the more amazing that while this is happening we are seldom aware of all that is going on. If this wasn't so, we would no doubt be confused due to the enormous bombardment of stimuli we routinely receive.

We take for granted many of the decisions our brains make about our behavior without seriously considering them. For example, a shaving routine is followed without cutting ourselves while thinking about other things. There are a multitude of things we hardly ever think about consciously, as our brains plan, organize, anticipate, categorize, choose, infer, solve simple problems, determine relationships, and make elementary decisions. All this is done in the absence of decision-making skills simply because no general class of decision making is needed. These things can be accomplished in accordance with our own practiced behavior along with our personal values and attitudes.

It is believed by some that a generalized set of problem-solving skills can be taught that is applicable to all situations. On the contrary, the way in which one problem is solved may not work for others. Many problems require specialized technical knowledge while others depend on a critical understanding of social implications. The process of solving problems from these different perspectives is ordinarily sensitive and personal and reflects an understanding of how we perceive ourselves and others.

Different problems don't have much in common and consequently no particular strategy could solve all of them. When we experience difficulty solving problems, it is rarely because we don't have specific problem-solving skills or can't skillfully think. More often it is because we don't have sufficient, appropriate data to consider. We don't know enough about the problem to consider all we must in solving it.

Thinking is not simply logical. We often use common sense to override logic. For example if we reach a conclusion that is believed undesirable, we change the premises or we manufacture a more acceptable conclusion. Thus, we make adjustments to accommodate value considerations. While thinking, a person may reach conclusions that others dispute, not because logic is lacking, but because different points of view are being expressed. This is evidenced by the persistence of so many profound religious, political, and scientific controversies among people with impeccable intellectual qualifications and manifest goodwill.

Higher-order thinking is not as rare as some educators believe. People in general are capable of higher levels of thinking and routinely engage in it as they plan, predict, monitor, evaluate, and question what they observe around them every day. Also, we repeatedly evaluate the consequences of our own thinking as well as the way others think.

Thinking effectiveness depends on students knowing what they are thinking about. They need adequate information. They also need to be unencumbered by structure. Thinking becomes difficult when learning is contrived, as is commonly the case in educational settings where teachers select topics for study. The most difficult kind of thinking is that imposed on us by someone else. This is because it is hard to provide explanations about things we have not reflected on in the first place, or to map out a decision-making route we have never pursued. Thinking is not a set of prescribed skills, but rather a natural process that is based on experience and that requires knowledge of the particular subject being pursued.

The primary task students have in school is memorizing information. However, memorizing is difficult when it is the primary purpose of a learning activity. Recall is greatly enhanced when it involves activities students find meaningful and the brain is employed as the individual wishes. Children are able to understand many complex things without difficulty in connection with pursuing their own desires, but find it burdensome to memorize information that is unrelated to their existing knowledge and interests.

When students fail to assimilate information, it is more likely due its lack of personal meaning rather than any intellectual deficiency on the students' part (Smith, 1990). Smith's conclusions about learning help elaborate the nature of the natural learning process and are consistent with constructivist theory and learning communities.

Chapter Six

Inquiry Learning

The learning strategy that is most consistent with constructivist theory is inquiry. This is because it features greater student autonomy along with encouraging curiosity as the means for generating questions to investigate. Also, in properly applying inquiry learning, the application of rigor in the research process is essential. Children don't naturally apply rigorous research standards to their investigations and consequently they often make erroneous conclusions from improperly obtained information.

Even so, as earlier explained, though students may have erroneous conceptions, the best hope for changing them is through students' own efforts to obtain meaning. Inquiry learning provides this avenue for clarification. The teacher's role is not to subvert students' curiosity, but rather to help students develop greater sophistication in their research along with the conclusions they make. Essentially they are taught to differentiate between questions that have merit and those that don't, as well as to engage in acceptably controlled experiments regarding the questions they research.

If student research is held to an adequate level of rigor, important concepts can be learned that are interesting as well as basic to the subject being studied. Caring teachers are interested in trying to see through their students' eyes, to struggle with them and their peers as they conduct their investigations, and to help them discover their own ways of making sense of the world.

It is important that students examine their work reflectively in order achieve greater cognitive development as they increasingly obtain more complex, complete understandings of abstract principles. The student's purpose is to take what he or she has learned along with classmates and interpret the world from as many vantage points as possible and gain insights not possible from a single perspective (Greene, 1988). As mentioned earlier, when students help direct their own learning, they can be expected to achieve a higher level of interest regarding important concepts and exhibit greater commitment for responsibly directing their own learning as well as contributing to the creation of a classroom environment that is conducive to productive learning.

In the process of working with their peers, all participants can be expected to acquire cooperative learning skills along with experiencing far better relationships than can be expected in traditional classroom settings. The world that students participate in now and in the future requires the ability to work successfully within social contexts, where shared meanings can be acquired and where a variety of interpretations of life experiences can be obtained, from which to more successfully apply what has been learned to the reality of an increasingly complex social world (Greene, 1988).

INQUIRY AND INTELLECTUAL DEVELOPMENT

Before students can effectively conduct meaningful, sophisticated research, it is essential that they have achieved an appropriate level of intellectual development. The nature of the research expected by teachers should be consistent with what children can actually do. Until the age of six or seven, children ordinarily are unable to really understand another person's point of view. They can manipulate symbols that represent the environment, but they are able to evaluate and understand only through direct perception.

From this time until they are about 12 years of age, children are in what is referred to as the concrete operations stage. This occurs after children have had sufficient experience in the environment to have accumulated and organized a store of fundamental concepts. At this stage, children require actual objects in order to process information about them. They cannot engage in abstract thought. During this time, the ability to conserve develops. This involves the capacity to retain a consistent view of such concepts as volume, length, area, weight, substance, or number while these are being manipulated and altered.

Thus, a child who is unable to conserve substance will think the amount of clay rolled between the palms of the hands and elongated has been modified in quantity. As they watch liquid from a container being poured into a differently shaped one, they believe the volume has changed. Without the ability to conserve area, these children are unable to understand that changing the outside dimensions of a rectangle does not necessarily change its area.

At about the age of 12, some children achieve the formal operations stage of intellectual development and consequently can formulate hypotheses and engage in deductive thinking. They are able to conduct controlled experiments wherein they discern possible confounding variables and arrange research strategies for setting all factors equal except the one in question. They also have the ability to engage in inductive thinking and draw conclusions that are based on research data.

In addition, children at this stage are capable of engaging in reflective thinking as they consider their own thoughts while simultaneously examining the thoughts of another person. They are able to analyze logical arguments and understand another person's point of view in comparison to their own (Piaget, 1970). At this stage students are able to address questions like whether or not the United States was justified in invading Iraq or whether it is possible to modify the influence of gravity on plant growth by such things as centrifugal force.

The question has often been raised regarding whether or not children actually achieve the various levels of intellectual development at the ages suggested by Piaget. The question has also been raised regarding whether or not all children eventually achieve the formal operations stage and become able to engage in abstract thought. Research has shown this not to be true. For example, in one study it was found that many adolescents may not attain the formal operations stage until their late teens or early 20s (Higgins-Trenk & Gaite, 1971). Fifty percent of the oldest group in this study, with a mean age of 17.7 years, had not yet achieved the formal operations level. Piaget later admitted that some individuals may attain formal operations as late as 20 years of age (Manaster, 1989).

It is interesting to note that most studies have found that only about 50 percent of adults are able to perform at the formal operations level (Jensen, 1985). Whether some individuals are inherently unable to achieve the ability to think abstractly or whether they would have attained this ability with more appropriate educational experiences is a question that is unanswered.

What this suggests to teachers is that they should avoid expecting their students to engage in particular kinds of intellectual activity at any particular time and realize that some students may not be able to do all that is required in the inquiry process. They might also operate on the assumption that with more experience solving complex problems they might eventually acquire the ability to engage in a formal operations level of thinking. At the same time teachers should be wary of holding students accountable for exhibiting such skills until they are able.

There are those who believe that an additional level can be justifiably added to Piaget's stages of intellectual development. It is suggested that the formal operations stage be renamed the problem-solving stage to differentiate it from a more advanced stage called the problem-finding stage (Arlin, 1975). Adding this stage is an acknowledgment that there is a significant difference between solving problems and insightfully finding problems to solve. It is concluded that isolating cogent problems is a different but higher level of thought. Certainly it appears that students find it more difficult to ascertain viable problems than to organize credible research strategies to investigate them. Yet both require abstract thinking capabilities.

INQUIRY LEARNING AND LEARNING COMMUNITIES

Inquiry is the primary learning strategy in learning communities. First, it allows students to investigate and solve problems that match their curiosities and that are more consistent with the problems they meet in the present as well as the future. Second, if students are helped to engage in research that is held to an adequate level of rigor, authentic information can be acquired that both satisfies their interest as well as being basic to the subject. Third, when proper teaching is applied, students can learn to apply research skills in the same way as experts in the field. Fourth, because students help direct their own learning, higher levels of interest can be maintained and greater commitment expected. Fifth, students are able to develop their intellectual skills far more than in traditional classrooms. Sixth, students can acquire information that is pertinent to a particular subject as well as personally meaningful. Seventh, students are able to secure far more sophisticated and useful social skills, ones that can be used throughout their lives. Eighth, students are able to develop far more advanced leadership skills than in traditional classrooms. Ninth, students are able to obtain a disposition to deal with life's problems in more sophisticated ways and thus become less likely to be unduly influenced by potential deceptions such as political statements, misleading advertising, and the like. Tenth, when students are engaged in meaningful, self-directed learning they are more likely to protect the learning environment from disruptive elements.

Unless teachers properly tutor them, students are prone to engage in inquiry investigations of low quality and little importance. Initially, students' inquiry efforts are likely to reflect their prior experiences in traditional classrooms where teachers ask most of the questions and students are simply expected to give answers. The kind of questions teachers commonly ask are apt to require simple recall rather than complex problem solving. Students, therefore, need to learn the difference between substantial questions and those of little consequence and unworthy of their time and effort.

In addition, teachers need to help ensure the conscientious participation of all group members. Students need to learn how to involve their peers in a meaningful way so that their interests are honored but their intellectual capacity is not exceeded. This can best be accomplished by all group members allowing other participants a requisite level of autonomy. Free choice is most likely the best fit for everyone.

In helping students identify questions for study, the teacher's role depends on how much experience students have had in the learning community. In the beginning, far more direction is needed. Eventually students become more self-directed. In the following dialogue, Mr. Fremont tries to help his students take on more sophisticated research than they at first proposed. This particular group of students has had several previous experiences helping their classmates focus on viable research projects:

Mr. Fremont: Class, Robert wants your input regarding research he is proposing for his study group. Would you explain it to the class, Robert?

Robert: My Dad went to the store to buy fertilizer for our new lawn and was told by the clerk that he needed to fertilize at least three times during the year. It was recommended that in the spring the fertilizer should be mostly nitrogen with a little potassium and phosphorus. The mid-summer application should be about the same, but in the fall he was told to apply less nitrogen and more potassium and phosphorus. I wanted to see if the salesman was telling the truth. We never used fertilize on our old lawn and it seemed to do OK.

Mr. Fremont: So what do you propose to do?

Robert: I thought we could go around the neighborhood and ask people what kind of fertilizer they put on their lawns and make a comparison.

Mr. Fremont: So, class, what questions would you like to ask, or what input do you have for Robert's group?

Mary: What kind of comparison do you plan to make?

Robert: We'll just try to decide which lawn is the greenest.

Kate: Don't you already know that those who fertilize will have greener lawns?

Robert: Well, I guess so, but I just want to see if the salesman was trying to put one over on my Dad. You know how that goes. I just thought he might be trying to sell more fertilizer. I wanted to find out how much is enough.

Randall: What makes you think that everybody has the same kind of grass? Maybe different kinds of grass requires different amounts of fertilizer.

Gordon: Yea, and what about the kind of soil people have? Some of them probably put on topsoil before planting grass and some of them probably laid sod. I wonder what kind of soil the sod farm has? I'll bet that makes a difference.

Carlos: What I worry about is how can you tell which grass is the healthiest just by looking at the color. And then there is the problem of making valid comparisons. How can you do that?

Robert: I was thinking that each member of our group could use a rating scale and then we could do observations and make comparisons.

Hazel: What about water? I don't think everyone provides their lawns with the same amount of water.

Robert: This looks like it's getting too complex.

Mr. Fremont: Don't get discouraged. Let's just get more input and see where it takes us.

James: One thing you could do is try to measure what's in the soil and arrange with the neighbors to let you water their lawns for the summer.

Robert: Mr. Fremont, what would you look for in the soil in order to make comparisons?

Mr. Fremont: Does anybody know the answer to that question?

Samantha: We had the soil around our house checked for salinity and alkalinity before putting in various plants. Some plants have a very narrow band of acceptable pH. And there are some areas around where the soil is salty. The man who checked our soil said it was quite alkaline and consequently we had to add some acid for some plants. Our area was once under the ocean and lots of limestone built up. It's alkaline except for a few places where evergreen trees have grown for a long time. They acidify the soil. That's what I learned in biology last year. That's why acid rain is not much of a bother in this area.

Ronald: You could do that, but what about the natural nutrients in the soil? Some areas around here are sandy and others have a lot of clay. Also, my grandfather told me that where sagebrush originally grew, the soil was much more fertile than in other places. He said some locations in our area are very fertile, while others are not. I don't know how you check for that. The sagebrush that used to be around here is long gone.

Mr. Fremont: So, Robert, how do you think you could deal with some of the problems that have been raised?

Robert: For one thing, it seems to me that we need to get some soil that is nutrient-free. That way we could regulate everything that's in there. Can you get something like that, Mr. Fremont?

Mr. Fremont: Yes, that can be done.

Tui: But Mr. Fremont, if we use that kind of soil, it won't be like anything around here and so our results won't say much about what we can expect naturally.

Mr. Fremont: That's right, Tui. But what can you accurately measure and conclude if you don't get some kind of control in your experiment?

Tui: Isn't there anything we can do to control if we use the stuff from the real world?

Ronald: I'll tell you what you can do. You can use different kinds of grasses that are already in place in the various areas of the neighborhood, but you can also plant these same kinds of grasses in the nutrient-free soil and carefully manage fertilizer and water. Also you can run your experiment during the entire year so that you can see the effect of the seasons. You might want to control the temperature or you might just want to expose all the samples to natural weather conditions. One way you get more control and the other you get a more realistic environment.

Robert: Now I'm starting to see more clearly what we can do so that we can really find out the best way to fertilize. But how are we going to get samples of different kinds of grass from various yards?

Sally: Look, we can get samples from each of our parents' yards. If anything is missing that we want to examine we could go looking for it around the neighborhood and ask if we can take samples. Maybe they'll let us do it in their backyards.

Robert: So the first thing we need is a sample from everyone's yard so we can classify it to see what else we need. We might need the help of Mr. Osterland at the plant nursery to see what kind of grass we have in our yards. What about the soil pH and salinity?

Mr. Fremont: We have test kits in our supply room. And you can test for more than just salinity and alkalinity. For example, the presence or absence of such minerals as iron could be checked.

Rick: So there needs to be a careful soil analysis. This is getting interesting. I'm more enthusiastic about this project than I initially was. I think our group can really find out something important.

Jerry: The way I see it, you need to get a number of samples from each yard you are studying. You need to expose each category of sample with the different treatments. I suggest you vary the kind and amount of fertilizer along with the time it is applied. This needs to be done with the nutrient-free soil samples too. Of course you need some control samples that receive no treatment except for watering.

Tui: How are we going to measure all this. Are we just concerned about how green the grass is?

Carolyn: Robert, you said earlier that the fertilizer salesman suggested your Dad change the proportions of potassium, phosphorous, and nitrogen for different times of the year. Did he ever say why to do that?

James: I know why they do that. They claim you need to feed the roots in the winter and then have more nitrogen to green things up in the spring. I guess potassium and phosphorous must make the roots grow. I think that raises another question, but it's easy to answer. All you have to do is measure how much root growth has taken place in plants that have been fertilized with potassium and phosphorous versus those that have not. Here again you might do it with all the different kinds of soil and grass.

Mr. Fremont: What about the greenness of the grass? How can that be validly measured?

Isaac: I think that's going to be hard. It seems to me that's not really what you want to find out. If the lawn is healthy, it should be green enough. I notice that in the late summer some areas in our lawn start to look sort of brownish even though the soil hasn't become too dry. I think it is just unhealthy because it has used up all the fertilizer in some spots and needs more. We hardly have to mow the lawn when it looks like that. One thing you could do is measure the health of the grass by how much it grows. I suggest you cut it about as often as people ordinarily mow and then measure how much you cut and make a summary of the total.

Mr. Fremont: So, Robert, are you clear about the questions you wish to investigate, and do you think you have a good picture regarding how to control for possible confounding variables and a valid way to collect the data you want?

Robert: I think we do. This is going to be a very exciting project. It's possible for us to make an important contribution to our community. I really like that. And I'm anxious to post what we find on our class Internet site. Maybe others might be interested in doing the same kind of experiment in their locations. Something like this probably needs to be replicated by others before too many conclusions are made.

In this example the teacher sets the stage for inquiry and invites students to help provide critical input. The students who are performing the experiment are directed by Mr. Fremont as well as their classmates to abandon a proposal that lacks sufficient rigor and to make sure that proper controls are put in place so that the results they obtain are valid. In this process, the entire class learns how to more carefully examine the questions being asked as well as how to more thoughtfully employ proper controls in an experiment. The experiment as it was initially proposed didn't contain a sufficiently sophisticated question to learn anything of value. Nor would the students involved have become acquainted with the way in which to make sure experimental procedures exhibit sufficient rigor. This example also shows how enthusiasm increases when students realize they can be involved in learning experiences of genuine value. It is evident that participating students have some knowledge and experience in dealing with learning of this kind. Before they have sufficient familiarity to provide this kind of help to classmates, teachers will undoubtedly have to supply some of the kind of input that students were providing. Teachers have to determine on the spot what their responses should be. They have to carefully observe what students are capable of doing, while at the same time helping them to increase in their capacity to engage in meaningful learning independently.

RESOURCES FOR INQUIRY LEARNING

Teachers need to prepare themselves for this kind of dynamic teaching. Because they are not following a carefully organized set of learning activities, what is needed at any point in time is unpredictable. One question that should be addressed is how teachers can prepare themselves to help students ask the right kind of questions when they don't know in advance what interests may be expressed.

Teachers should avoid just providing questions for students to research. At the same time they need to know a rather large list of potential researchable problems in the area. Well-prepared teachers will have already created a list of potential research questions to which they can refer as they interact with students. Of course, they don't just give the students access to this list. Instead the list simply provides a background for teachers out of which they can lead students toward asking their own questions. Without such a list, teachers will find it hard to provide students the necessary cues to finally settle on questions to research. An example list may include items like the following:

- How do politics frame political speeches during campaigns for the presidency of the United States?
- What is the relationship between governmental decisions and world history?
- What has been the role of religion historically in creating or solving problems in the world?
- What is the history of changing temperatures in the world historically? What is the most likely scenario currently?
- What is the impact of chronic fatigue immune dysfunction syndrome (CFIDS) on society? How does this influence the way in which the medical profession deals with this disease?
- What are the different possible causes of depression? What is the relative effectiveness of talk therapy versus antidepressant drugs?
- What is the nature of individuals' responses to controversial questions that they have no way of correctly answering given the small amount of information available?
- What is the relationship between temperature and the amount of daylight during the day for leaves to change color and drop from their trees?
- To what extent do literary authors' life experiences influence the plots of their novels?
- To what extent have artists validly anticipated coming events in the world and incorporated it into their paintings?
- What is the impact on animal behavior of different kinds of music?
- To what extent do authors have an agenda they are trying to communicate to their readers apart from the story line in their novels?

Another source of ideas for student research can be found in a variety of periodicals. For example, in history students may consult journals like *Historical Research, History Today, American Heritage, American History*, and *Current History*. In science they may wish to consult *Scientific American, Science, Discover, Smithsonian*, and *Science News*. In other subjects they may find the following periodicals to be of help: *Natural History, Weather-wise, Weather, Archaeology,* and *Psychology Today.*

There are many other periodicals with varying amounts of sophistication that students may consult. Sometimes these materials are available in public libraries, while others may only be available in university libraries. Where learning communities have been implemented it is wise for school libraries to obtain subscriptions for some of these references.

It is also helpful if schools provide students with computers as well as science laboratories. Schools might also have arboretums, greenhouses, and garden plots where students can engage in research on a long-term basis. The research materials needed for student involvement in learning communities is far more vast than that ordinarily provided in traditional schooling. In some cases, availability of resources can be greatly expanded by receiving dona-tions from various commercial companies in the area. Some companies wel-come the opportunity to support the schools in this way.

Inquiry-oriented instruction within learning communities provides a greatly enhanced environment for promoting higher-quality student ques-tions as well as a much more enlightened process for thoughtfully answering them (Scardamalia & Bereiter, 1992). In addition, community-based learning helps students become more ardently involved in their research, consistently applying evidence in scholarly ways and logically developing arguments regarding their findings. This process becomes increasingly sophisticated over time (Engle & Conant, 2002).

One especially positive outcome of learning communities is for students to be more inclined to respectfully help each other and learn from each other. They also demonstrate increased productivity, student ownership, and cogni-tive engagement (Crawford, Krajcik, & Marx, 1999; Ebers & Streefland, 2000). It is significant that students who participate in learning communities exhibit better content retention, are more flexible while working in hypothet-ical situations and counterexamples of research, create more novel ideas, employ more complex forms of argumentation and explanation, more suc-cessfully transfer knowledge to other domains, are more capable of summar-izing complex explanations, and become more adept at determining what constitutes valid evidence in support of research findings (Brown & Campi-one, 1994b).

Once students have completed their research, it is necessary for them to prepare written reports and to make detailed presentations to other students in the class. This instruction is not just to demonstrate their own understand-ing, but also to increase their peers' understanding. Consequently, students are encouraged to teach other class members with the purpose of having them understand the research questions and strategies along with what was learned and the conclusions that seem warranted. All students should have the benefit of learning as much as possible from the research of other groups.

This also provides teachers an opportunity to continually assess the intellectual development of their students and determine ways to provide more appropriate support.

Teachers should always remember that students' abilities to formulate valid questions and conduct carefully controlled experiments depend on their intellectual development. Thus, different levels of sophistication can be expected from different students. This is the reason teachers should carefully monitor the research process, so they can make sure students don't expect more of each other, or of themselves, than they should.

It may be difficult for students who can engage in abstract thinking to have the requisite patience for their peers who find it impossible to think in terms of multiple causation or probability. Yet these students' participation in research should not be unnecessarily restricted. Obviously there is always the risk of their limited capabilities encouraging negative feelings, but their participation also has the potential for fueling their growth. It is hoped that with proper teacher intervention these students experience an increase in their intellectual capacity.

In addition to this, inquiry learning can provide a way for students to more fully understand the social, historical, artistic, political, and physical worlds in which they live and acquire skills with which to perpetually enhance this understanding. Inquiry learning provides a format for students to consistently satisfy their inherent desire to investigate their world, understand it, and use this knowledge for their unique purposes. Students also discover that through inquiry they can learn in ways that are consistent with their natural inclinations and discover information that is personally satisfying and that bears far greater utility than that obtained in traditional learning formats.

In order to provide students with the resources they need to conduct their research, teachers must collect a lot of materials such as periodicals and other printed materials, Internet sites, videos, and addresses of various social and government agencies. Where available, students may benefit from access to various libraries outside the school along with university personnel and members of various occupations. In some cases, students may gain access to such sophisticated equipment as electron microscopes and the like.

Chapter Seven

Relationships and Communications in Learning Communities

Good relationships are a central aspect of discipline in learning communities. If students fail to acquire a true sense of care about each other there is little hope that moral development will occur and that autonomous responsibility and resultant good classroom behavior will arise. Without good relationships, learning communities simply do not function. Because students must learn together and share in the various learning tasks, it is critical that they help create an environment that embodies cooperation and encourages them to truly look after each other.

In traditional schools student relations are not deliberately promoted. Neither are they intended to be a part of the curriculum. Students are not usually taught what constitutes good relationships and how they might benefit from them. In fact, student interactions are often seen as a menace to the instructional process and discipline as well as a threat to evaluation.

As previously mentioned, traditional schooling consist mostly of students listening to lectures and privately working at their desks (Goodlad, 1984). Interaction is discouraged because it rarely has anything to do with instruction. Ordinarily it consists entirely of students' social agenda. Consequently teachers usually consider association with classmates to be a waste of time. But it should be noted that such distracting student conversations occur primarily because of disinterest in the prescribed curriculum and because students are commonly deprived of social interactions.

Also, because students may not be intrinsically interested in classroom learning and committed to doing what is assigned, they are easily distracted by any alternate agenda and may actually be looking for something besides the assigned learning activities to occupy their time. Under these conditions, students disengage themselves from teacher expectations and often become disruptive.

In addition, tests are nearly always a private matter. Any sharing of information is considered cheating. This is because tests are used primarily to compare and sort children. It is assumed that making achievement comparisons on a common schooling agenda is more important than the learning and social benefits associated with students working together on learning projects.

RELATIONSHIPS IN LEARNING COMMUNITIES

Each learning community depends on wholesome relationships in order for its members to properly define their work together. All participants have to engage in the process of community building for the end result to be a true representation of their wishes and aspirations. When caring relationships are sought as a primary ingredient of a learning community, the needs and desires of members can more fully be met. Members are more able to collaborate with each other and share their work and learning as well as help in the process of creating a group identity. A group identity must include a strong commitment to community purposes along with acceptance and caring by all community members.

The Components of Caring Relationships

Relationships are based on interpersonal agreements about a set of obligations concerning the ideals and ideas the group members hold in common (Wickett, 2000). Because the primary agenda of the community is helping group members fulfill their needs, relationships are mutually reinforcing. Members learn that their own well-being and that of their peers are intertwined. In helping their associates accomplish what is important to them, students are much more fully satisfied than otherwise possible. This is because many of their personal desires are social in nature.

Though they may at first focus attention on gratifying individual desires, eventually the desire for satisfying interpersonal needs exceed the desire for those that are strictly personal. Children thus learn that nearly all of their needs can best be satisfied within a social context. This is an eye-opener for most children, due to the fact that the bulk of their previous efforts have been devoid of interpersonal need satisfaction. They mistakenly believe that they have to give priority to fulfilling personal needs. Many times this involves thwarting the needs of others, as it is commonly thought that need-fulfillment is a competitive process. Turning this erroneous idea around is one of the important challenges of community building.

Relationships in learning communities reflect kinship and love along with duty and acceptance. For this to happen, teachers must treat their students as if they were their own children. Perhaps the central feature of this association is the willingness of teachers to extend to students the highest level of personal autonomy which they are capable of responsibly applying.

Obviously the amount of autonomy offered students will gradually increase as they gain experience working in a caring way with fellow students and assuming increased control over their own learning. It is inappropriate to thrust greater autonomy on students before they are prepared to assume it. Yet there may be a tendency to do this when students prematurely ask for more decision-making opportunities.

As pointed out in a previous chapter, in determining the proper time for providing greater autonomy, students should not have to prove they are sufficiently responsible before being given more decision-making power. Rather, caring, knowledgeable teachers help students acquire greater control over their own learning as an integral part of the community-building process. Thus, children help decide when they are ready to assume more autonomy. In addition, mistakes should not be held up as proof that students are not ready for greater self-determination. Rather, students should be encouraged to examine mistakes and help decide their implications for future decision-making responsibilities.

Promoting Caring Communities

Better relationships are created by pursuing common interests. Group members should examine all potential learning activities for their collective significance according to community values. These should be consistent with community goals along with the group moral code, but conducive to helping all members entertain personal interests as well.

In a properly operating learning community the common good is always consistent with the collective good of all its members. Nobody's needs are simply ignored for so-called greater purposes. Personal interests can and should be pursued in connection with achieving group purposes. All needs can be successfully attained through active interaction and collaboration (Glickman, 1993). In reality, the result of caring teaching is the broadening of the curriculum and the enhancement of individualization (Smith & Parrish, 2003).

For the sake of enhanced relationships, difficulties and conflicts that arise in a learning community should be considered without reference to universal rules. The specifics of the situation should dictate the decision-making process along with conclusions reached. Most problems have unique circumstances requiring unique solutions. Even problems that appear to be similar should not be handled in a routine way. Different circumstances or the involvement of different people may dictate a unique approach. It is also critical that group members do not come to think of similar problems as being the same. The group mindset should be toward examining each situation on its own merits with the distinct possibility that different solutions may be appropriate.

Better relationships are also encouraged when members value each other more than their separate achievements. Students should not look toward personal accomplishments as a way to mark themselves and fellow group members in order to determine relative worth. This, of course, is the way worth is determined in traditional schools, with devastating consequences (Covington & Beery, 1976). When love and acceptance depend on one's achievements, children do not feel the steady flow of care that is necessary for relationships to grow and flourish. Children's sense of worth and approbation is subverted when they have to perpetually satisfy conditions for acceptance.

The roles of students in a learning community should not be too strictly defined. There needs to be a good deal of latitude in which children can determine their own roles. Stereotyping creates narrow expectations, which interfere with personal flexibility, and relegates learning roles to preset requirements that greatly limit personal growth. Learning communities prosper when students are able to experience a spirit of inquiry and achieve personal satisfaction by defining their own unique roles in the community.

Student relationships are enhanced when the means of learning are just as important as the ends. Focusing on ends is particularly destructive, especially when comparisons are made between students. The learning process itself must be valued and not considered as merely a way to achieve grades. Focusing on ends puts students at odds with each other. Rather than promoting the welfare of others, the practice of emphasizing the ends of instruction encourages students to avoid cooperating with each other and perhaps even to sabotage the learning of classmates.

Student relationships need to be close and informal as well as cooperative. Members associate with each other for the intrinsic value of these associations, not because of the personal use to which such associations may be put. Acceptance and love are the business of learning communities. The uniqueness of each community is forged by the ties students have and the kinship that develops through working on common interests and sharing in the excitement of learning. These associations help to satisfy social as well as personal needs and give a great deal of meaning to life in a democratic society.

The sense of community predictably evolves by students sharing common experiences. Through this means they generate a compact of mutual obligations and commitments out of common purposes. This helps students develop a sense of care for fellow participants and provides a way for them to acquire the social skills necessary for fruitful relationships (Sergiovanni, 1994). These are key to group functioning and the quality of learning.

Building community appears to require the development of relationships that foster the growth of a common mind, which consists of shared values, conceptions, and ideas about schooling and about the human experience. It is difficult to communicate unless there are shared beliefs, values, commitments, and even emotions. These basic conditions are not easy to achieve in a diverse population, but can be developed through more potent, caring relationships. Until good relationships are developed in a community, problems can be expected. It is difficult for people to inherently care for others who are radically different with respect to race, culture, ideology, and theology (Noddings, 2002).

In promoting better student relationships, acceptable common purposes must be pursued. Teachers need to help their students examine various possibilities for learning projects that represent interests the group has a strong desire to pursue. The direction for learning must be clarified and consensus attained. Otherwise the commitment needed to promote significant learning and resultant relationship development will not be achieved.

When students work successfully together, a value framework evolves that allows learning activities to take on special meaning and significance. Through these experiences the school is transformed from a common workplace to a sacred enterprise—sacred in the sense that the work done there has special significance and importance to students and is recognized as the genesis of satisfying, caring relationships. Through this means students come to recognize the value of their associations and realize that their school community has unique, special significance.

What makes this kind of experience unparalleled and motivating is the way students come to feel about the importance and legitimacy of their purposes and how these desires properly represent broader social values and principles that are central to what school achievement should be (Sergiovanni, 1990).

When learning communities reflect respectful relationships, the vision and covenants shared by the group become operative. The common value dimension needed for extraordinary student performance evolves and students become enthused about common hopes, dreams, needs, and interests as well as about the values and beliefs of everyone who has a stake in the school. The desires of parents and other interested parties coexist with those of the school.

All participants ultimately acquire a vision of what the school stands for and tries to live up to. This drives students learning toward community purposes and a high degree of satisfaction and accomplishment (Brandt, 1992). They respond to each other as a covenant community with associated agreements, which are entered into as binding, solemn commitments for which trust is essential.

This process of consensus building binds students together around common themes that embody a sense of mission and group ownership (Sergiovanni, 1990). As previously pointed out, present-day schooling reveals a near vacuum with respect to mission (Goodlad, 2000). Students consequently are denied opportunities to become energetically involved in legitimate schooling experiences that articulate with their own learning proclivities and purposes and promote an ethic of care.

ENHANCING CARING RELATIONSHIPS IN LEARNING COMMUNITIES

The ability of children to successfully relate to teachers and peers depends on the environment in which they live. Problems at home contribute heavily to school-related difficulties (Duncan & Brooks-Gunn, 1997; Erickson & Pianta, 1989). Children must have had successful relationships at home for them to readily engage in meaningful social discourse and achieve a real sense of self-reliance and autonomy. Self-reliance and resultant successful social experiences are based on both the child's previous history of adult support for exploration experiences and the extent to which classroom teachers provide a secure base for exploration (Pianta, 1999).

To promote better relationships between themselves and their students, teachers must learn to read children's nonverbal signals accurately and appropriately respond. Teacher responses should convey acceptance and emotional warmth, offer assistance, model caring behavior, and help children to feel comfortable in governing their own behavior.

The Teacher's Role in Promoting Caring Relationships

Research indicates that students value teacher relationships that make them feel worthwhile, support their independence, motivate them to achieve, and help them interpret and cope with environmental demands (Pianta, 1999). Teachers can improve relationships when they express an interest in learning about students' prior experiences. They need to find out what is important in their students' lives, what they like about relationships, where they have found success or failure, and what they like or dislike generally. They also need to avoid episodes of control (Greenberg, Kusche, & Speltz, 1991).

Also, they must be willing to spend one-on-one time with students to help them deal with issues that are too sensitive for public disclosure. This is a difficult task in traditional classrooms, but private conversations can routinely be provided in learning communities. In these sessions, teachers should convey the message that they are available and interested in students. Students need to feel they are accepted and that teachers can help them with problems they face. Teachers should convey the message that they are readily available and can be counted on as a source of safety and comfort and a reliable resource for problem solving.

When children believe it is safe to communicate sensitive issues with their teachers, they are much more willing to openly express themselves. The result is for understanding and relationships to be greatly enhanced. In order to promote more caring relationships, it is often recommended that students stay with the same teachers for several years (Smith & Parish, 2003).

Perhaps an even more daunting challenge is to encourage students to form caring relationships with fellow students. Unfortunately, many young people not only fail at developing a capacity to care, they seen unable to understand what it means for others to care for them (Noddings, 2002). Some even confuse coercion with care. Others believe they are being cared for when in reality they are being exploited. Many have simply given up on the hope that anyone will ever care for them.

According to Noddings (2002), to care is to be engrossed with others in a special form of attentiveness that involves a motivational shift from the person offering care toward the needs of someone for whom they care. Children who are genuinely cared for detect evidence for this in the expressions and behavior of those around them. Unfortunately, many are unlikely to find this at school. That is the reason teachers need to genuinely care for their students and teach all members of the learning community what it means to really care about someone else.

In order to show they care, teachers must learn how to give their undivided attention to their students. This should be combined with sufficient intimacy that children feel they are special to their teachers. Teachers should not only repeatedly demonstrate their care, they should help students understand what it is and promote it in all aspects of teaching and learning. Learning communities cannot survive without genuine care developing between students.

The Use of Praise in Caring Relationships

In expressing care, teachers should be wary of indiscriminately offering praise. Praise is erroneously thought to indisputably help children improve their behavior and achieve at higher levels. Interestingly, most teachers automatically praise, without considering the existence of certain negative repercussions. However, praising students for their accomplishments can be harmful. Statements such as "Good boy, James," "Way to go, Helen," and "Nice work, Rolaine" promote dependency, evoke defensiveness, and create anxiety.

Children who are given this kind of evaluative praise feel compelled to satisfy both explicit and implied desires of others, rather than feeling inclined to pursue their own aspirations. Eventually, their sense of well-being can be compromised (Ginott, 1971). A better strategy is for teachers to help their students appraise their own performances and then acknowledge that the student assessments are valid.

Praise can cause negative reactions by children. For example, children (1) may have witnessed praise being delivered just before criticism is given, (2) may realize that teachers offer praise in order to draw attention to some students they wish them to imitate, (3) may mistrust the sender and their credibility, and (4) may conclude that the praise-givers cannot be relied upon to be truthful because some praise is designed to simply make them feel better even after they have failed (Tauber, 1999).

Praise doesn't help children solve their problems, nor does it help them deal with negative feelings they confront when they experience failure. But should children be praised for particularly praiseworthy performances in school? As pointed out earlier, this is ordinarily a bad idea because adults usually fail to help students attribute their success properly. For example, they may unknowingly allow children to attribute their success to luck rather than effort, preparation, or ability. Teachers may fail to help students see that their success is under their own control and is the result of their own efforts and expertise.

When students mistakenly attribute their success to luck, or lack of success to fate, their ability to visualize how success is really achieved may be undermined. This may make them inclined to avoid responsibility for what happens to them. Teachers should also avoid attributing success to ability because effort is often a more likely determinant of success. When students believe their success in the classroom is at risk, their relationships with others predictably deteriorate.

Teachers should avoid praise that students can interpret as a condition for love and acceptance. Teachers commonly praise students for complying with rules or doing their schoolwork. This seems benign enough in terms of any harm it might do, and behaving properly and conscientiously doing assignments seems to be a good thing. However, when following a teacher's instructions garners praise, children usually get the mistaken idea that this is required for teacher approval. To counter this tendency, teachers should express acceptance and appreciation to students for reasons other than good behavior or academic excellence.

As indicated earlier, in trying to satisfy parent and teacher expectations, some students become over-strivers. Students who are thus affected are driven by the assumption that the sole measure of personal worth is school accomplishment. These children become bedeviled with meeting high academic standards because parents and teachers expect them to excel and because in the past they have repeatedly proven they are equal to the challenge. Unfortunately they conclude that school excellence is equated with personal worthiness. They believe that it is only when they achieve excellence academically that they can be loved and accepted as they wish.

When parents and teachers witness such excellent performances, they often increase expectations. This is a signal to students to elevate their own expectations in order to continue receiving the approval they have grown to irrationally crave. Eventually these youngsters do not require others to raise the standards. They do it themselves automatically and eventually create standards so high they cannot achieve them. At this point they may realize they have about reached their zenith and consequently stand in jeopardy of losing the status and acceptance they so desperately crave.

Ironically, the plight of these children goes unnoticed. After all, they have habitually done well in the past. What's there to worry about? Unfortunately these students eventually arrive at an unforeseen conclusion. They live in terror that they might not be able to achieve the next escalation of expectations. Success thus becomes a fearful specter that can immobilize them and create anxiety and depression. To be successful, they must elevate their achievements above their assumed level of capacity. Shockingly, when they find themselves faced such insurmountable expectations, some even go so far as to end their lives (Covington & Beery, 1976).

COMMUNICATION IN CARING LEARNING COMMUNITIES

Relationships in learning communities are particularly sensitive to the nature of communications, given the fact that their quality depends extensively on thoughtful interactions and a willingness to engage in provocative discussions. Learning groups depend on discussions that convey meaningful insights in a caring way. Members must tune into the various ways information is transmitted. Usually this data is conveyed by the spoken word, with some being expressed through nonverbal cues and innuendos. Care that is conveyed by the spoken word needs to be supported by appropriate nonverbal information. An expression of love and acceptance that is not accompanied by appropriate nonverbal gestures often is interpreted as insincere.

When learning community participants try to create a caring atmosphere, it is critical for them to understand the nature of their own statements along with those of their associates. Otherwise transactions fail to go smoothly and learning is thwarted. Early on it is expected that communications may be confrontational and ineffective and only involve those willing to risk being discredited. At this point, discussions are likely to involve only a few group members who tend to consider topics in a bland, superficial way (Mercer, 2002).

Communication Influences

Most of us are unaware of the source from which our communications emanate. Ironically, we sometimes say things that may be offensive even when there are no conscious hostile intentions. Yet many of our statements are made without realizing where they come from. This makes it all the more important that we learn the source of our utterances so that we might more conscientiously monitor and control them.

It has been discovered that all our experiences and associated feelings are permanently recorded in our brains and are automatically called forth by stimuli in the environment. The responses we make and the feelings they generate are not necessarily meant to hurt anyone. Yet our intentions don't necessarily direct these communications. They arise spontaneously just as they were recorded earlier in life unless the individual makes a conscious effort to modify them (Penfield, 1952).

From the point of view of Transactional Analysis, messages we convey to others come from life experiences and are recorded in the form of three ego-states: Parent, Child, and Adult. Each of these ego-states is defined by a unique, consistent pattern of verbal expressions and associated feelings (Berne, 1966). Information in each ego-state is retained in the brain both in conscious and unconscious forms.

During daily activities, many of our verbal expressions arise as if from nowhere, without any conscious thought, as does any feeling associated with experiences that give rise to these expressions. Interestingly, our statements are well articulated and purposeful and appear to have been carefully formulated, and they are expressed as if we just turned on a recording machine. Thus, information recorded long ago is simply played back. Words and feelings are articulated as they were once learned and require little or no conscious effort to produce (Berne, 1966).

Parent Ego-State

Berne explains that the Parent ego-state consists of a recorded collection of events experienced during the first five years of life. This assemblage includes the pronouncements heard from real parents or parent substitutes. These experiences are recorded in an unedited form. When children are young, they have no way of assessing whether or not what their parents say is appropriate. Therefore, if the parents were malicious or hostile toward their children or toward one another, their conduct is recorded as it occurred without the benefit of interpretation and revision.

Also recorded is the emotional information associated with parents' expressions. Sometimes children are exposed to traumatic experiences from the very people on whom they depend for sustenance and love. Some children have been excessively abused. Children have no way of dealing with any extenuating circumstances that may surround what they observe. They are unable to engage in the necessary abstract thinking that is essential for interpreting their observations. It is common for children to interpret parental hostility as being directed at them when it is not. They fail to understand that parents' animosity may have been aroused by someone other than themselves.

The Parent ego-state is a repository of all the admonitions, rules, and laws proclaimed by parents and other adults during the growing-up years. This store of information is not just composed of verbalizations. It also consists of voice tones, facial expressions, and recollections regarding physical contact. Included are the many denials issued regarding children's requests along with the controlling *no*s and *don't*s with which children are commonly bombarded as they attempt to satisfy their curiosities and explore and understand their world.

New experiences do not erase these recordings, even if they are contrary. They remain and continue to constitute the person's history. Thus, positive nurturing later in life does not erase the reality of previous abuse. However, the individual is not simply helpless and unable to modify how he or she responds to others. Modifications can be made to expressions that constitute more reasonable and socially acceptable forms (Woollams & Brown, 1979). This requires conscious awareness of the nature of what has been recorded in childhood and diligence in suppressing the negative and expressing the positive.

Despite this, individuals find that many ways of feeling and responding automatically emerge unless they learn to control them and remain conscious of the tendency for them to be expressed without careful screening. For example, if your mother employed various ways of making you feel guilty whenever you failed to meet her expectations, it is likely a sense of guilt arises whenever you confront circumstances where you might have failed or are accused of doing so. An emotional response not unlike that suffered as a child under duress ordinarily emerges along with excuses and explanations regarding why you should not be blamed.

This emotional baggage tends to be automatic and the verbal responses routinely cloaked in justifications and efforts to shift the blame to others. Every accusation seems to require reverse accusations be made. Obviously, acting upon negative experiences from childhood can greatly hamper successful relationships in learning communities.

The Parent ego-state also includes the smiles, hugs, and expressions of pride and delight of parents, grandparents, teachers, and other important adults, and the contexts in which their approval was given. Later on, similar experiences will again produce positive feelings. Affirmative experiences are critical ingredients of happiness and are associated with more compatible relationships with others later in life. For children to acquire an adequate sense of well-being they should receive these experiences in abundance.

As children grow, they record the complicated, well-intentioned platitudes and precepts to which they are subjected—pronouncements of which they have only a vague understanding. They also have no way of judging the validity of these statements. They may hear adults make expressions like the following: "Associate only with people of your own kind," "Never tell lies," "Clean up your plate," "Eat your dessert last," "The idle mind is the devil's workshop," "You can never trust a cop," and "Haste makes waste." Admonitions like these are judged by adults regarding their validity and moral appropriateness. With young children, however, they are simply regarded as true and are rigidly internalized and used as patterns for dealing with others. Many of these attitudes continue on into adulthood and become sources of conflict between people.

Child Ego-State

The Child ego-state is simultaneously recorded along with the Parent and consists of responses children make to what they hear and see. Most of these reactions are emotional because of children's limited ability to really understand the meaning of language. The Child ego-state is much like the Parent in terms of the strong influence these experiences and emotions have on verbal transactions later in life. When an individual has an experience that is much like something experienced in childhood, similar emotions emerge. The result is for individuals to lose emotional control and act irrationally. Communications and consequently relationships can be adversely affected.

Adult Ego-State

In early childhood, the Adult ego-state begins to emerge. In the beginning, it is very fragile and subject to injury and distortion, particularly when there are too many commands coming from the Parent and too many fears emanating from the Child. If this occurs, the Adult ego-state may have limited capacity to validly interpret and regulate feelings and expressions from the Child and Parent ego-states. The result is for children to find difficulty telling the difference between life as it was taught and demonstrated to them, life as they felt it or wished it or fantasized it, and life as they figured it out for themselves.

When the Adult ego-state is not distorted by abuse, it can scrutinize rules children have recorded from the Parent and determine their trustworthiness for current applicability and judge whether or not they should be rejected. At the same time, the Child ego-state can be analyzed in order to determine whether feelings that have been stored are acceptable or simply inappropriate reactions to the Parent. This investigation does not automatically erase deceptive behavior that emanates from the Parent or Child. Rather it provides a way to restrict their influence and helps construct more trustworthy interpretations of transmitted information and more wholesome expressions of emotion.

Learning communities find it difficult to withstand the unbridled emotions that come from an out-of-control Child ego-state. It is likewise hard to foster relationships in an atmosphere of platitudinous, distorted expressions that emanate from the Parent. Reasonable people find them offensive or perhaps amusing, while those who express them may fail to understand why others reject what they say.

Learning communities depend on how successful members are in determining their own internal state as well as that of others involved. Each individual must attempt to discover the internal state of other participants and learn to adeptly interpret their statements and emotions. How can this be done? Internal states are partly revealed by the verbal information transmitted by peers as well as by teachers. There are also nonverbal cues that are useful. Facial expressions, gestures, and voice inflections can sometimes provide clues regarding which of the ego-stages is being expressed.

Evidence that the Parent is involved might include putting hands on hips, folding arms across the chest, clucking the tongue, sighing, pointing the index finger, wagging the head, furrowing the brow, pursing one's lips, tapping one's feet, or looking disgusted. The Child is likely being expressed through tears, temper tantrums, complaining, pouting, a quivering lip, shrugging shoulders, giggling, squirming, laughter, or downcast eyes. Finally, the Adult ego-state appears as smiles of approval and looks that ask for more information to be given.

It is wise to help students assess verbal information as well as nonverbal cues in deciding which ego-state is active. Taken together, they help to illuminate situations that may be difficult to truly understand otherwise. In making assessments, each individual needs to be cognizant not only of others' behavior, but also their own. In doing this, everyone should be careful not to attribute negative intentions to others. Remember that much of what comes out of these ego-states is inadvertent.

Verbal expressions emanating from the Parent ordinarily are in the form of demands, commands, and reprimands. Essentially they are created to control and direct others. They often embrace criticisms and labels. The following examples illustrate Parent statements:

- Get to work now.

- No one is to leave their seat until the bell rings.
- You must clean up your lab table before you can leave.
- Who said you could go to the pencil sharpener?
- You never turn your homework in on time.
- If you weren't so lazy you would have finished your research a week ago.
- When are you going to start coming to class on time?
- You cause me more trouble than anyone else in class.

Verbal expressions displayed from the Child ego-state usually are in the form of uncontrolled emotion. These may vary from expressions of extreme elation to uninhibited disgust. For example, the student might say:

- I hate this class. Your rules are so unreasonable.
- You never tell us when we are going to be tested.
- I refuse to work with Ralph. He stinks.
- Roberta never does her share of the work on our project.
- How can you expect us to do 50 problems in one night?
- I sure like it when we learn about how diseases are transmitted.
- Wow, I finally understand how to work these problems.

In contrast to the Child and Parent, the Adult ego-state is thoughtful and rational. Ordinarily it is represented by requests for information and takes on a role of moderating the negative impact that comes from the Child and Parent when they are not constrained. The following statements illustrate this:

- What is your plan for finishing your project?
- What have you and Bryce done to resolve the disagreement you had during our discussion yesterday?
- What additional materials will you need to complete your research project?
- How do you plan to evaluate the quality of your work this term?
- Tell me about the conclusions you have reached on your project.
- How much time do you need to make your presentation to the class?

Applications in the Classroom

It is easy to detect the differences between the ego-states, particularly when one remains in the Adult ego-state. The Adult is orientated toward understanding others and cooperating rather than simply reacting in an emotional or controlling way. It is, therefore, a much better way to promote fruitful interactions and encourage satisfying relationships as well as to avoid discipline problems. Teachers need to explicitly teach the nature of the ego-states and help students recognize them in themselves and others in order to ensure their interactions are productive. Both teachers and their students must remain in the Adult ego-state (Harris, 1967).

Without teacher guidance, students are likely to engage in unproductive classroom talk and even indulge in interactions of a negative nature. Steering the class toward caring, productive interactions can only be accomplished when teachers avoid Parent-oriented directions, which unfortunately seem to be habituated in the behavior of many teachers. Watkins (2005) has identified various ways students can learn to engage in interactions that are productive rather than filled with negative emotions. In the following examples, a discussion purpose is listed along with an example of an associated question or response that supports students engagement in fruitful interactions and helps them avoid negative content while promoting an attitude of care:

1. Focus on meaning:

   a. Reasoning is explicit: "I think what you saw is a function of the way light is reflected from the surface of the surrounding water."
   b. Others are invited to examine one's reasoning: "Now that you have listened to my idea, what do you think of it?"
   c. Inquiries are made into another's reasoning: "I've listened to your explanation, but I need you to tell me more about how you came up with that idea."
   d. The perspective of others is voiced: "What you're saying seems to show that the conclusion we reached is not consistent with the data we obtained in our research."

2. Moderate conflicts:

   a. Tentative language is used: "It's possible that I've drawn the wrong conclusion about global warming and its impact on the earth's human population."
   b. Assertions are viewed as hypotheses to be tested: "I've been thinking that the response made about the estimated distance between the two lights in a dark room may depend on who is present as well as the size of the group."
   c. Similarities as well as differences are acknowledged: "Now that I see the additional evidence I understand that your point was well taken."
   d. Disagreements are framed in terms of ideas, not persons: "It seems that killing the Kurdish people with poison gas was an acceptable reason to believe that Saddam Hussein had at least one weapon of mass destruction in his military arsenal prior to the Gulf War."

    e. Multiple stances are assured: "Given what we have learned about the asteroid that hit the earth near the Yucatan Peninsula and the enormous volcanic eruptions in India, it is clear that there is more than one possible explanation regarding the extinction of the dinosaurs."

3. Advances the learning group together:

    a. Further inquiries are proposed for the group: "We could try to figure out exactly where the pollution comes from by more carefully analyzing the water collected from the river and looking for other possible sources."
    b. Changes of position are mentioned: "In hearing what you said about different sources of global warming and the genesis of the Ice Ages, I see things a bit differently."
    c. Mutual goals are emphasized: "I think if we discuss our research design further we will be able to organize our research so that all confounding variables are controlled."
    d. Enhancement of communal knowledge is sought: "It is critical that we examine any relationships possible between both Clark's and Lee's research before we draw any final conclusions."

The examples cited above are far different from what is normally expected in the classroom, but they illustrate the kind of interactions that teachers should promote in learning communities. Obviously, complex thinking and discussions are promoted along with good classroom relationships. Students don't inherently understand the nature and importance of this process and consequently need to be explicitly taught how to interact regarding classroom content that can potentially produce conflict.

A thoughtful atmosphere in a properly run learning community provides caring interactions even when conflicting assertions are made by class members. Students learn that caring interactions regarding clashing information can help them increase their understanding of complex, potentially troublesome issues.

In learning communities considerable cross-talk is needed between various research groups along with periodic reports being made to the entire class. Through cross-talk, each group benefits from the research and input from others. During these interactions, clarifying questions can be asked and unique observations made. This helps everyone concerned acquire a deeper understanding of all learning projects currently underway. Often, needed insights can be obtained that make a real difference regarding learning approaches and the conclusions reached (Brown & Campione, 1994a).

Many times interactions of this kind can greatly heighten the sophistication with which students approach their research and consequently enhance the results and understanding they obtain. When groups meet together, they routinely address new ideas, consider strategies that show promise, deal with difficulties encountered and determine what others think can be done about them, achieve special insights about the group learning process, and ascertain how group members feel about what they are learning.

The teacher's role in learning communities is always in transition from greater to lesser control as students become more comfortable and able to responsibly direct their own affairs and communicate caringly and effectively. Initially, teachers focus on building community, communicating effectively, promoting relationships, assisting students as they organize their learning projects, and helping members determine the basic principles for regulating classroom affairs and student conduct. In the beginning, much of teachers' time is occupied explaining the details of the community concept, giving feedback, and creating questions for students to consider.

At the same time, teachers should focus on an ethic of care and model various academic roles such as coming up with researchable questions, formulating research strategies that control for confounding variables, conducting research, drawing defensible conclusions, and preparing reports. They also model leadership, which they will gradually turn over to their students (Watkins, 2005).

Chapter Eight

Democratic Discipline in Learning Communities

Democratic Discipline in Learning Communities depends significantly on the proper implementation of learning community principles. When learning communities are properly employed, discipline can be completely integrated into the teaching–learning program. Discipline problems are dealt with by the class in the same manner they handle any other classroom problem or deliberate regarding the learning projects they wish to undertake.

Because students may initially be unfamiliar with agency principles and how to apply them in group situations, the teacher must provide a lot of coaching and offer instruction about how democratic discipline operates in connection with students' participation in a learning community. Thus, students learn about the operation of a learning community in the process of constructing one in their classroom, while at the same time dealing with any potential discipline problems. This makes it unnecessary to employ a separate discipline approach that in all likelihood would be inconsistent with the operations of the learning community.

Classroom meetings are routinely held in which decisions are made regarding learning desires and opportunities, along with solving problems about classroom procedures and discipline issues. Within this context, issues regarding learning responsibilities are addressed. Students have an opportunity to express themselves regarding their needs and how they can best be realized within the learning community. Any event or action that could thwart their learning is discussed and actions taken to prevent it. Thus, students together deal with potential discipline problems as well as any that have recently arisen.

Because of the caring atmosphere that exists in learning communities, students are encouraged to deal with problems not only sensitively but also forthrightly. Problems must not be allowed to proliferate unresolved. In this atmosphere, student autonomy is supported within the context of shared purposes and learning objectives. Thus, the teacher does not perpetually direct efforts to eliminate discipline problems. Rather, students are taught how to deal with the problems themselves and allowed to follow through as necessary.

Because student needs are part of the substance of learning communities, they are much more likely to be fulfilled than in traditional classrooms. The result is for fewer discipline problems to emerge. The whole framework of learning communities provides an effective format for children to avoid most problems and helps solve any that do occur.

Perhaps the most critical feature of democratic discipline is the lack of routine teacher intervention in dealing with discipline problems. For the sake of democratic principles, they must become dedicated to allowing children to eventually solve their own problems. Thus, teachers do not step in and punish or provide logical consequences for classroom disruptions. These are handled in the ongoing democratic processes that are characteristic of learning communities.

Many adults have no confidence in children being able to solve their own discipline problems. However, when they intervene, student ownership is subverted and discipline problems magnified. When teachers attempt to curtail student wrongdoing, they often encourage students to make a game of misbehaving. To some it becomes a challenge to somehow outdo their teachers. In other cases, students turn against their teachers and become determined not to learn. Some students withdraw while others are reinforced by teachers' punitive actions, and their misbehavior consequently increases in frequency.

Teachers are often perplexed by the complex and seemingly illogical responses of students to their punitive actions. However, they are quite predictable. Unfortunately, many teachers think punishment can be completely defined as actions they take to control students' misbehavior, with a predictable increase in productive school work and cessation of disruptions. However, this ordinarily is not what happens. As mentioned earlier, some students find the intended punishment to be reinforcing. Teachers should avoid the trap of believing that what they intend to be the effect of their behavior is exactly what will occur. Rather, student responses must be used to ascertain these effects.

Allowing students to be more self-directed ordinarily has far more predictable outcomes than punishment. When classroom government is gradually turned over to students, they become more enthusiastic and proficient in monitoring themselves and eliminating discipline problems. In the meantime, teachers should not impose punishments nor mete out so-called logical consequences (Beihler & Snowman, 1990).

Discipline issues should be addressed in regular classroom meetings, where from the start students are taught to manage their own classroom behavior. In the beginning, discipline issues are likely to be regular topics for discussion, with the teacher gradually becoming less active in helping students define how to regulate their own behavior. The teacher's role is to provide counsel as needed and raise necessary questions as students attempt to deal with potential classroom disruptions. A teacher may, for example, ask students to reassess their efforts to apply consequences to each other as the result of misbehavior when this practice is plainly inconsistent with democratic principles.

Reassesssments are likely to be necessary because of students' previous experiences in the schools, in which punishment and consequences were routinely imposed for almost all classroom infractions. In doing this, teachers should avoid giving too much direction. Their task is to raise questions, not provide solutions. They are more effective if they initially provide the insights of an experienced adult until such time as students learn how to apply democratic principles more effectively themselves.

As teachers increasingly provide students more autonomy, they will gradually accept more responsibility for their decisions and actions. When students routinely address discipline issues in classroom meetings, a set of appropriate classroom procedures can be expected to emerge with which all are comfortable. These procedures look nothing like the lists of rules ordinarily imposed on students in the school. The results are more consistent with the special requirements of a learning community.

Employing democratic discipline in learning communities is the format chosen because it best lends itself to learning the practical aspects of democratic living. Unfortunately, schools are commonly more like dictatorships than democracies. In such an environment, students lose an opportunity to learn how to live successfully in a democratic society.

Learning communities also provide learning conditions that are more consistent with human nature, along with supplying more need-satisfying experiences for students. Traditional schools generally fail to provide the means for student needs to be fulfilled, nor do they supply experiences that are consistent with students' natural way of learning. In learning communities a more caring environment is created in which students can become involved in more satisfying relationships with their peers and learn much more about getting along and becoming productive members of society.

In learning communities students learn how to communicate more successfully and to direct their own lives. Their education becomes more gratifying because they are able to acquire a necessary sense of independence while operating successfully in a need-satisfying social environment. Because they are committed to others, they become oriented toward the common good and become beneficiaries of covenants and shared values, which help them feel like contributing members of society.

Under these conditions, students are much less likely to act out in frustration and instead work successfully to solve problems that arise. Students who are involved in learning communities obtain a valid belief that they are working on and solving real-life problems. They no longer are frustrated by what many believe are meaningless tasks imposed on them in traditional schools.

PREVENTING DISCIPLINE PROBLEMS

Discipline in learning communities is almost exclusively a function of conducting an insightful instructional program oriented toward intellectual inquiry and making sure that discipline issues are approached in the same way as such instructional concerns as group social dynamics, leadership, relationships, care, the validity and usefulness of research proposals, evaluation strategies, student and teacher roles, procurement of learning resources, expected excellence, need fulfillment, cooperation strategies, students' interests and learning desires, occupational directions and how they relate to the curriculum, values and commitments, and the nature of the covenant.

All of these principles and procedures should be employed appropriately. Most especially student involvement in learning communities must involve a requisite degree of autonomy, combined with group identity and responsibility. In order to ensure the prevention of discipline problems, any issue that may relate to potential difficulties should be brought up in regular classroom meetings.

At times there may be problems that involve individuals or small groups that require privacy. When student privacy is an issue, or when only a limited number of students need to be concerned, small group meetings should be held accordingly. For example, a student who fails to participate appropriately in his or her study group because of parental abuse may need a private conference with the teacher so that the student can be properly protected as well as avoiding the embarrassment that may come from an open meeting.

Obviously it is much better to prevent discipline problems than waiting until difficulties emerge. Teachers should become skilled at predicting potential problems. For example, rude comments most likely spawn reactions that lead to full-blown conflict. Students' failure to complete their learning commitments in coordination with their learning group predictably courts uncomplimentary comments. Because of concerns regarding these possible consequences, they should be addressed in classroom meetings and the class allowed to discuss them in detail until everyone is satisfied regarding how to prevent problem situations.

Many teachers worry about making sure that all classroom time is used for instruction and may feel discussions dedicated to preventing discipline problems to be a waste of time. However, such efforts are appropriate. In reality, they help make more time available for learning. In traditional classrooms, an inordinate amount of time is commonly devoted to solving discipline problems that could have been prevented. A rather substantial amount of instructional time is usually lost while teachers try to bring disruptive situations under control. Often their reactions effectively promote more disruptions. Had more time been devoted to preventing problems initially, less inappropriate behavior would have arisen.

Teachers should feel comfortable using whatever time is necessary to implement a preventive discipline program. It should help in a comprehensive way to avoid most problems. However, follow-up meetings need to be held during the year to help reinforce and clarify potential difficulties that have been identified and to address problems not anticipated.

In classroom meetings, an atmosphere of care should be created. In addition, teachers should make sure that students' needs are part of the deliberation process. The nature of learning should also be considered in any decisions made either about discipline or the instructional program. Undergirding all discussions in classroom meetings should be a devotion to democratic principles and adherence to the covenant.

Preventive Discipline and Punishment

Ordinarily teachers punish students who violate classroom rules. Sometimes this is done systematically by such practices as putting the names of rule violators on the board. Having your name put on the board is ordinarily meant as a warning. After this, each successive infraction of the rules results in a check mark being placed on the board beside the name. Ironically some students are just disruptive enough each day to get their name on the board but no more.

Sometimes students make a game of being disruptive by agreeing to take turns being unruly in class. They disturb class just long enough to get their names of the board and then go back to work. The result is for the chalkboard to be filled with students' names, but with no punishment meted out. As previously mentioned, some students are reinforced by punitive teacher actions. Their motives may be to get attention, take revenge, or compete with the teachers for power. In any case, punishment has been shown to often be unsuccessful in modifying poor student behavior (Englander, 1986).

Despite the fact that the negative effects and ineffectiveness of punishment have been known for years, it is unquestionably the most used kind of discipline. Kohn (1993b), for example, reports that children who are punished commonly resent those who punish them and reduce the output of academic work. In addition, punishment usually fails to curtail the kind of behavior it is designed to eliminate.

Research shows that punishment leads to three possible outcomes: calculation of risks, blind conformity, and revolt (Kamii, 1991). Children who engage in risk calculation try to determine how they can get away with disruptive behavior or avoid something they consider unpleasant. Children who blindly conform are filled with fear and in the process fail to take chances and grow. Their wills are broken and they have an inclination to accept what they are told unquestioningly, including slogans and propaganda, and are prone to drawing illogical conclusions (Kamii, 1984). Children who revolt openly oppose their teacher's influence.

Obviously, teachers should think twice before punishing their students. More often than not teachers simply react to student misbehavior in a negative way without thinking of the consequences. It should also be noted that even when punishment is systematically employed, negative effects are still the outcome.

For punishment to be even minimumly effective in curtailing disruptive behavior, a number of associated conditions must be simultaneously met. First, proper timing has to be employed. Punishment must be administered at the onset of misbehavior. As little as 12 seconds' delay tends to render punishment relatively ineffective (Aronfreed, 1968). Even when children are trained to obey rules, they disobey them if they observe their peers doing so (Walters, Parke, & Crane, 1965). Thus it appears that for punishment to be effective, it not only must be dispensed soon after misbehavior is observed, it must also be administered consistently to every individual who violates rules.

The intensity of punishment and the complexity of associated classroom tasks also influence the effect of punishment. An example of a complex classroom situation is the conditions under which students are allowed to talk. For some classroom activities, no talking is permitted, while in others it may actually be encouraged. Sometimes talking is not encouraged but is tolerated, as when students are working in small groups. Students may be confused about how to respond in different situations due to the fact that expectations may be vague and even administered inconsistently. When it is simple for students to discriminate teacher expectations, severe punishment is more effective, while in situations requiring greater discrimination, milder punishment is more productive (Aronfreed, 1968; Azrin & Holtz, 1966).

It has been found that when the intensity of punishment is increased gradually over successive administrations, it is unlikely to suppress misbehavior. Thus, punishment is more effective when it is sudden and substantial. Interestingly, punishment escalation is ordinarily practiced by most classroom teachers. They start out administering mild punishment and gradually increase intensity as students resist their influence. Ironically, the Supreme Court in its 1975 decision on punishment supported escalation as an appropriate technique by mandating that punishment must first be less abrasive and that it can then escalate into paddling (Azrin & Holtz, 1966).

The effectiveness of punishment is also influenced by its frequency. For it to be effective, every instance of misbehavior must be punished. When punishment is administered periodically, misbehavior continues unabated until the individual anticipates that it will soon reoccur. To be proficient, teachers have to maintain constant monitoring of every misbehaving student in class and administer punishment consistently in every case (Englander, 1986).

It is clear that suppressing misbehavior with punishment is a very complicated affair involving several factors. No single factor ensures effectiveness, and their administration must comply with strict conditions. In addition, the effects of the various aspects of punishment are additive. Consequently, to really work effectively, punishment must be administered expertly, incorporating a number of critical conditions simultaneously. Interestingly, even under these ideal conditions, one can expect only about half of the students to comply as punishments dictate (Englander, 1986). Obviously, under these conditions profitable learning is unlikely to occur. Given the complexity of most classroom situations and the inability of teachers to conform to even minimum expectations in delivering punishment, it is doubtful that anyone could punish effectively.

It should be pointed out that reducing the incidence of misbehavior is only part of the issue when appraising the effects of punishment. Punishment can promote aggressiveness, reduce learning, cause withdrawal, increase misbehavior, and promote poor teacher–student relationships. It can also inhibit spontaneity, cooperativeness, and assertiveness, along with moral development (Burden, 1995; Curwin & Mendler, 1988). Ironically these side effects can occur even when students only observe others being punished (Kounin & Gump, 1961).

Preventive Discipline and Logical Consequences

Applying logical consequences is often given as a more benign way to deal with student misbehavior. Supposedly it makes sense to children that a logical consequence is deserved, while punishment may be judged as too harsh and excessive. This is one of the critical but misguided assumptions about logical consequences. Unfortunately, children often interpret the administration of logical consequences as punitive. Keep in mind that when situations are open to personal interpretation, as they are in this case, students all routinely make unavoidable mistakes in perception.

It can be expected that children have a different interpretation of a logical consequence than the one assumed by the teacher. For example, a teacher may inform a student who is routinely out of his seat that he has a choice to either sit in his seat or have it removed. A child who can see no reason that he should be confined to his seat for long periods of time may consider this as having no choice at all. He sees no reason that he shouldn't be able to stand at his desk during class and considers the possibility that the teacher would remove his seat as punishment.

One of the key tenets of logical consequences is to give students a choice rather than forcing them to behave as directed. As the previous example illustrates, however, the child may not see it as a choice. Thus, the child's interpretation may not be the same as the one intended by the teacher and therefore the logical consequence may not actually exist in the mind of the child.

Other examples of supposed logical consequences include the following:

- If a student shoves someone else on the stairway, the teacher would inform the student that he or she can decide whether to avoid pushing in the future or go back to class and wait until everyone else has cleared the stairway before being allowed on it.
- If a student turns in an incomplete paper, the student may be told that it won't be read unless a completed paper is submitted.
- In the event students write on the classroom walls, they would be required to either clean them or pay the janitor to do it for them.
- If students fight during recess, they may be barred from recess until they provide the teacher with a plan regarding how they propose to avoid fighting in the future.
- When students are late for class, they may be told to either come on time in the future or wait at the door until they receive a signal from the teacher that their coming late will no longer disturb the class.
- If children are late for dinner, they may have a choice to be on time in the future or be sent to bed without any food.
- When children tip their chairs back against the wall until they are resting on only two legs, they may be told they can either place their chairs on four legs or have the front legs permanently blocked up.

In each of the above logical consequences there is room for misinterpretation and for an inappropriate distinction to be made between logical consequences and punishment. Take for example the case of children who are late for dinner. It seems to be a more logical consequence in this situation for children to fix dinner for themselves. But even then they may interpret this response as punishment, though the parent may not.

In applying logical consequences to misbehavior, it is common to provide children a choice between two competing, and perhaps equally aversive, consequences. The result is punitive control. This is particularly so when there is a whole range of possible consequences from which only two rival alternatives are selected. It is difficult to communicate to students that these consequences are not simply punishment. To children they may appear to be arbitrary, equally punitive choices.

The way teachers' actions are interpreted by their students is far more important than what teachers intend. For example, a teacher may ask a student to leave the classroom as a logical consequence for talking out during a lecture. This is likely the same as the punishment they have routinely suffered in many other classroom situations.

To a limited degree consequences may seem logical to students when they have been involved in determining what the consequences will be. When they help decide on the consequences for particular misbehavior, in advance, they hopefully will accept them as appropriate. But, even then, if they find the consequences to be painful, they will be inclined to rationalize the seriousness of their misbehavior, try to justify it on some grounds, and believe the consequences to be excessive and thus punitive. Of course some students may find consequences to be reinforcing, causing an increase in their disruptiveness.

Preventive Discipline and Rewards

Not only do adults try to influence children's behavior with punishment and logical consequences, they also attempt to shape them with rewards. This approach is rarely criticized. There seems to be nothing wrong with reinforcement techniques when the result is less disruptive behavior and more productive learning. But rewards also have their downside. As outlined in a previous chapter, the more they are used the more they seem to be needed to sustain appropriate behavior (Kohn, 1993b). Thus, though children may be inclined to learn without being rewarded before rewards are established, afterward they are likely to refuse to learn without them.

Extrinsically rewarded students are also less likely to pursue optimal challenges, display inventiveness, and perform under challenging conditions (Koestner, Zuckerman, & Koestner, 1987). They become less interested in the learning tasks for which they have been rewarded (Deci, 1981; Lepper, 1983). Rewards are devastatingly effective in suppressing enthusiasm for activities children might otherwise enjoy (Kohn, 1993b). More than 100 studies verify the fact that extrinsic rewards diminish intrinsic motivation (Ryan & Stiller, 1991).

Researchers have found that the greater the incentives offered students, the more negatively they view the activities for which they are given (Freedman, Cunningham, & Krismer, 1992). They even come to dislike what they must do to be rewarded. They apparently see it as an obstacle to what they wish (Kohn, 1993b). It isn't even necessary for a student to be rewarded to be turned off learning. Simply watching others acquire rewards can have a temporary motivation-killing effect (Morgan, 1983). It is insightful yet regrettable to acknowledge that students may come to loath learning in school in consequence of being rewarded for it.

Rewards also adversely affect the quality of what students do. Students who are rewarded become less-sophisticated learners. As they focus on obtaining rewards, they tend to overlook what quality involves. Performance improvement occurs only on extremely simple—indeed mindless—tasks, and even then the improvement is quantitative (Kohn, 1993b). Rewarded students choose easy tasks, are less efficient in using available information to solve novel problems, and tend to be illogical in their problem-solving strategies (Condry, 1977).

Of all the ways children are led to seek rewards, perhaps the most destructive is to limit the number of rewards available. This, of course, describes school grading precisely. As can be expected, in the minds of many students, grades replace learning as the primary purpose of schooling. Grades are valued by students for their own sake, and the excellence they are supposed to represent and encourage is sacrificed to obtain them. When this is the case, cheating is cultivated and a strain between teachers and their students created.

Reward systems ordinarily require careful monitoring of student behavior. Interestingly, when children are monitored as they work on a task, they tend to lose interest in it, possibly because they interpret the surveillance as controlling. This occurs even when no reward has been offered (Harackiewicz & Manderlink, 1984). Apparently the use of both surveillance and rewards comprises a double dose of control, and together they accelerate the loss of self-determination and interest in accomplishing the task being rewarded. Used in conjunction with each other, surveillance and rewards have more negative effects than either does alone (Lepper & Greene, 1975).

Even though the usefulness of rewards as motivators has been vigorously debated through the years, a recent meta-analysis has confirmed the conclusion that virtually every type of tangible reward actually undermines intrinsic motivation. In addition, threats, deadlines, directives, and competitive pressure diminish intrinsic motivation because students interpret them as efforts to control. Choice and self-direction, on the contrary, are intrinsic motivators (Deci, Koestner, & Ryan, 1999; Ryan & Deci, 2000a). It should be pointed out that these conditions exist only when students are offered rewards in advance. The same effects don't apply when reinforcers are administered without students expecting them. Of course, in most cases, teachers try to entice students by offering rewards in advance.

Preventive Discipline and Learning Principles

In establishing a program for preventing discipline problems, teachers should help their students understand the difference between the learning principles they will establish and the list of rules commonly imposed on students by their teachers. Classroom rules are ordinarily a statement of teacher expectations in the classroom, and consist of such items as "raise your hand if you want to speak in class," "all assignments must be turned in on time," "keep you eyes on your own paper during exams," "keep your hands and feet to yourself," "don't talk during quiet study time," "follow directions exactly," "don't fight," "ask for permission to use the pencil sharpener," "never leave the class without teacher permission," and "always bring your textbook, paper, and pencil to class."

Students are used to these kinds of rules. Most have a long history of having such rules imposed on them. Ordinarily they have no role in creating classroom rules, and consequently some students routinely oppose them. Such lists of rules have no place in learning communities. Instead, students help direct their own learning and behavior management.

Given their previous experiences in the school, students initially need help in creating learning principles. The principles students help create should be designed to accentuate learning. That is their purpose. Thus, each principle defined should be directly related to learning purposes and effectiveness. The following list provides examples of learning principles and associated questions that teachers could use to initiate discussion about the particular principle:

- Question: How can we as a class ensure less interference during learning interactions with each other? Principle: Everyone needs to carefully listen to each other during class discussions to avoid disrupting the communication process.
- Question: What kind of learning experiences will most effectively satisfy class expectations? Principle: The class needs to engage in learning that attends to student preferences, provides for their needs, and is varied, challenging, and enjoyable.
- Question: How can the class best support everyone involved, given the fact that groups of students will be working on different projects at the same time? Principle: Class members need to engage in their learning activities in a way that does not interfere with the learning of other groups.
- Question: What are important characteristics of the kind of relationships desirable in a learning community? Principle: Proper relationships involve respect for everyone's feelings, ideas, interests, and beliefs. All class members should be proactive in this endeavor.

- Question: What kind of learning format is likely to be the most beneficial for achieving important class objectives? Principle: Investigating questions and solving problems through inquiry provides the best means for acquiring relevant knowledge and experience in the classroom.
- Question: How can members of the class be prepared for the kind of learning desired? Principle: Students should come to class with questions, ideas, and sufficient background information to engage in meaningful discussion about potential learning projects and with suggestions about how to carry on valid research on viable topics.
- Question: How can class members pursue agreed-upon learning opportunities and acquire meaningful understandings of critical knowledge? Principle: Class members should maintain a focus on educational objectives and avoid being distracted.
- Question: How can students benefit from the learning of other class members? Principle: Students should learn conscientiously and cooperatively and share their thoughts, ideas, understandings, concerns, difficulties, opinions, and research findings with other class members through discussions and reports.
- Question: What should we as a class do about mistakes made by class members? Principle: Mistakes are a normal part of academic experiences and serve to advance learning. Students are free to make mistakes without criticism and use what they learn to refine future learning.
- Question: What should students do if they discover in the process of completing their part in a learning project they become interested in a new direction? Principle: Students are free to take new directions in their learning after they have discussed their new desires with their learning group and acquired their input about new proposals. The issue to be resolved involves the implications of not completing responsibilities initially made and what should be done about them. Students should also explore how the new direction fits into the overall learning goals of the group.
- Question: What should you do if you disagree with members of the learning community? Principle: Members of the learning community should feel free to courteously question the contributions made by others as well as receive critiques regarding their own work.
- Question: What should be the nature of interactions with other members of the learning community? Principle: All members of the learning community should feel that they have sufficient opportunity to speak and be heard, contribute and be taken seriously, and express their feelings and be accepted and respected.
- Question: What principle should be used to guide the actions of members of the learning community? Principle: All members of the learning community should be provided with sufficient autonomy to set their course of

study and manage themselves within the realm of community commitments and benefits.

- Question: What should be the role of the teacher in the learning community? Principle: The teacher needs to raise questions and point out issues that must be considered in establishing learning projects and managing classroom behavior. Teachers should serve as examples in conducting their own research and sharing the results with their students.
- Question: What information should the teacher provide about the operation of the learning community? Principle: The teacher needs to provide instruction about the operation of the learning community and help ensure that it works properly. All components regarding learning communities must be carefully articulated and applied.
- Question: What should be the teachers' role regarding leadership in the learning community? Principle: The teacher should provide an example of appropriate leadership and help students assume significant leadership roles as they become increasingly able.
- Question: How should responsibility be defined in the learning community? Principle: The success of the learning community depends on assuming collective responsibility. At the same time each individual is responsible for his or her role in conducting learning obligations and making sure they support rather than interfere with the activities of other students. Responsibility especially involves strict allegiance to the covenant shared with group members.
- Question: What kind of an atmosphere can best serve the purpose of the learning community? Principle: An atmosphere of care should be promoted in the learning community. Each individual should look out for the interests of fellow members, support and defend them regarding their actions inside and outside the classroom, and make sure that the learning atmosphere in the classroom supports the learning process for everyone.

Preventive Discipline in Practice

The nature of discussions regarding the prevention of discipline problems by forming learning principles is similar to those engaged in to create learning proposals, execute them effectively, and evaluate outcomes. A few of the learning principles listed above are incorporated into the following discussion of a teacher with one of his classes:

Mr. Adams: Over the past few days we have been discussing your learning projects in considerable detail. Each of you belongs to a learning group and I assume you have initiated your research. To expedite your plans we need to discuss classroom procedures or learning principles that hopefully will help you in your learning quests. One issue that needs to be addressed is the possibility that something that happens in class may interfere with your learning. How can you as a class ensure less interference during learning interactions?

James: We need to stay out of the way of other groups.

Rochelle: I don't see how we can do that. To do our research, we need to move around the room and get the supplies we need. We can't avoid each other.

Carlos: That doesn't need to create a problem. We can just stay out of each other's way and go about our business.

Genene: That's easy to say, but in my experience when people get moving around the room there is always a lot of noise. Kids poke at each other and throw things.

Samuel: That doesn't have to happen. In this class we could just agree not to do that. We were able to agree about our learning projects. Why couldn't we do the same thing about noise and stuff?

Mr. Adams: It sounds like Genene and Samuel disagree about whether or not you can regulate yourselves when it comes to involvement in a number of learning projects which require you to move around the room.

Carolyn: Well, I think we can do whatever we set our minds to. There is no reason we can't just stop goofing around while we're learning. But I see another problem. We may sometimes talk so loud in our groups that it disturbs others.

Ralph: We can regulate that too. Isn't it possible for everyone to just stop talking so loud?

James: I've seen how that works. You start out being quiet. Then someone in one group gets a little loud and others do the same. Soon members of all the groups have to talk loud just be heard.

Mr. Adams: It sounds like you're saying that it is impossible for us to control ourselves if someone else talks too loud.

James: I didn't mean that exactly. That's just what I've seen happen.

Kulei: We can be just as quiet as we want to be. It's just a choice we make, and any of us can keep from being too loud.

Brian: I agree. If we make up our minds to keep a good learning atmosphere in the class we can.

Cheryl: But what if someone gets too loud and doesn't want to stop?

Lois: We just have to agree to remind each other and then remember that we have agreed not to be disruptive.

Ronald: That is all well and good. But what if someone repeatedly talks too loud?

Carol: I say they should be punished. That will put a stop to the problem.

Mr. Adams: What do you suppose will be the result of punishing someone for talking too loud?

Kulei: I think they will just become angry and cause more trouble.

Robert: That's for sure. I've seen that happen a lot. I don't think we should punish anyone for talking too loud unless we just want more trouble.

Carol: What are we going to do then? We can't just let them stay in the class. We have to get them to stop somehow.

Mr. Adams: Let's find out how many of you are committed to keeping the classroom sufficiently quiet that we can successfully communicate with each other. What about it class? (All raise their hands.) If you are being noisy, what would you like to see happen?

Rochelle: I'd feel alright if someone just told me. But what if there are a number of people talking out during a discussion or just being too noisy while we are working on our projects? Mr. Adams, couldn't you just stop class and tell everyone to be quiet?

Mr. Adams: That is something I'd like to avoid. Like I explained when we were determining what your learning projects would be, you need to decide for yourselves what you believe will be the most effective way to maintain a democratic atmosphere and still protect the classroom learning environment.

James: I think we need to help each other know when we're being too loud. It may take a while, but if we courteously remind each other, it will soon be OK. We could talk about this in a week or so and determine how we think it is working. We could make other adjustments at that time.

Mr. Adams: How many think that's a good idea? (All indicate they do.)

JoAnn: I want to bring up another issue. I have been meeting with my group for about a week now. I agreed to take on part of the project that seemed interesting to me at the time. After getting into it, I've discovered that I'd rather focus my attention on something else. I haven't told the group how I feel. I wanted to have the whole class discuss it first. I need to know if it's alright to change what I'm doing midstream.

Mr. Adams: What about it, class? What do you think about JoAnn's dilemma?

Carvel: I think once you commit to something you should stick with it. You shouldn't just dump your responsibility anytime you see a different way to go.

Tiffany: But what if you can make a more important contribution to the group?

Carlos: I think the group should talk about it and decide what they want to do. Group members shouldn't just do whatever they want. But it might be a good thing to change something if it seems OK to the whole group. The person who wants to make a change should talk to the group and show them how what they want to do is better that what they decided earlier.

Lois: I agree. I think we should be looking for ways to improve what we do. We have to be able to use our judgment when we see more promising new directions to take. We have a responsibility to the group to do that.

Robert: I sort of agree with that. But I worry about taking too many new directions. We could lose sight of what we originally planned. Maybe a lot of critical things wouldn't be investigated and there would be holes in our work. Who is going to do the work that is abandoned?

Kulei: That's just the chance we should take. We can't let original plans dictate all we do, especially when during our work we see new things to do that are very important. Some of what we initially decided may best be abandoned, particularly if something better is pursued.

Samuel: But what if all the individual wants to do is have an easier path to follow?

Cheryl: I think it's worth risking that. I don't believe it's an issue so long as the person pursues something that all agree should be done.

Carlos: So if the group doesn't agree with the change someone wants to make, it can't be done. Is that right?

Carolyn: Maybe people should be allowed to continue the original commitment with the possibility that later they may change what they are doing. Maybe the person should be encouraged to continue examining a new direction until they find good arguments to present to the group.

Samuel: That means they would have to double up on what they are doing. I think their work would suffer if they take on too much.

Ralph: I think they should be able to do it if they want. We shouldn't try to make sure everyone's work is the same. We'll all do different amounts of work. If I was really interested in doing something, I would spend the extra time. It's worth it to me.

Mr. Adams: I see most of you shaking your heads in agreement. Is this what you would like to do? (The class agrees.) For a few minutes I'd like you to turn your attention to another matter. What do you think should characterize our relationships with each other?

Brian: That's easy. We should be courteous with each other.

Mr. Adams: So, what does that mean?

Carvel: I've been the object of teasing in some of my classes. I think that should stop.

Tiffany: We should take turns to talk. We shouldn't interrupt each other.

Genene: I think we should talk to each other with respect. If we truly respected each other we would talk in a different way than many of us do.

James: Maybe we need to help defend each other whenever discourteous things are done. When someone is disrespectful, there should be a reminder given. Wouldn't that be your job, Mr. Adams?

Mr. Adams: What do you think?

Kulei: Given how this class is organized, I don't think it's Mr. Adams responsibility. It belongs to all class members. Besides, if we are all committed to being courteous, we can look after ourselves.

Mr. Adams: You've talked about what you would do in class. What about outside the class? What if you observe members of our class being treated discourteously elsewhere? What if someone was being bullied? What if you discover a member of our class who is singled out for ridicule on the Internet?

Lois: That happened to a friend of mine when I was at another school. They took pictures of her in the shower and spread them all around school. Her whole family eventually moved. If someone would have supported her and reported it to the school principal, the perpetrators would have been the ones embarrassed.

Cheryl: We can't let things like that happen. We have to look after each other no matter what or where it happens. I'm embarrassed to say I didn't report a bunch of bullies that beat up on someone a couple of years ago.

Ronald: I hear a lot of derogatory remarks made in the halls. Maybe we could also get that eliminated. We could start by sticking up for members of our class.

Mr. Adams: If you seriously accept this responsibility, you'll find school to be a much more pleasant place. I am aware of some extreme problems with bullying that have occurred over the years. Had students like you taken the responsibility to deal with them, there would have been a lot less suffering. I want to offer my support for what you have decided today. Sometime in the near future let's get together and make an assessment of what we have decided to do.

CORRECTING DISCIPLINE PROBLEMS

Despite efforts to prevent discipline problems, there are inevitable difficulties that arise that require attention. Some of these problems require a reaffirmation or clarification of earlier commitments. Others occur because certain particulars were not anticipated and addressed in advance. When discipline problems occur, they are put on the agenda for consideration in classroom meetings. The purpose of these meetings is to help students understand how to solve discipline problems and eventually prevent them. The goal of teachers is to help their students learn to not only regulate learning, but also to monitor and direct their own classroom behavior. In doing this, students soon acquire a sense of ownership and are able to effectively solve classroom discipline problems.

Corrective Discipline and Classroom Meetings

In classroom meetings, students learn to deal with discipline problems without resorting to either punishment or logical consequences. They come to understand the detrimental effects of these tactics along with the problems associated with rewards. They are able to appropriately apply these principles to the classroom when their teachers promote understanding within the context of the ongoing instructional program.

Ordinarily it takes some time for students to see the value of non-punitive classroom procedures, given the fact most of them will have experienced these tactics exclusively in their schooling up to this point. In addition, they are used to having teachers impose these tactics on them and often have developed associated responses that are personally detrimental. They have not had experience cooperating with their peers in order to help govern themselves.

Eventually students realize that there is no virtue in punishing each other and simply take upon themselves the responsibility of self-regulation in order to achieve what is most desirable in the classroom. In due time, teachers will find it unnecessary to monitor student behavior, and any inclination to impose punishments and consequences will be eliminated. In these circumstances, students find that learning has its own reward and that self-regulation empowers them and helps promote a desire to achieve excellence.

Corrective Discipline in Practice

Let's look at an example of how a learning community might deal with a particular discipline problem that has emerged despite earlier efforts to avoid such problems. In this case, Alice has come to Mr. Adams, her teacher, complaining that in their learning group there is no shared leadership. She explains that Blair always takes over and runs things. Mr. Adams agrees that sharing leadership is an item that should be discussed in a classroom meeting so that all students could become more able to perform successfully in leadership situations. At the same time he cautions Alice regarding problems that could emerge if her learning group's situation was specifically identified as having a problem. He tells her that it would be better if neither she nor another group member publically identifies the issue, but rather lets it come up in a discussion of related issues. He explains that it would be appropriate if Blair is the one to bring it up within the context of a general discussion about the issue. The following is an example of what might happen in the next classroom meeting:

Mr. Adams: Class, a few weeks ago we discussed the way in which leadership should be shared in learning groups. It's time now to make an assessment regarding this important aspect of group learning. Recall that it is considered essential for all group members to learn leadership skills. Let's have you share your impressions regarding this important aspect of learning communities.

Colleen: I've really learned a lot about leadership that I didn't know before. I've never been able to do it before. Now I see that it is a huge responsibility. You have to avoid interfering with other students' learning responsibilities while at the same time making sure things get done. And you have to coordinate things too. Then there's the problem of arbitrating disagreements. We haven't had a lot of that, but have been successful resolving problems. I think we've all been able to learn a lot about that. We've all taken over leadership for a time.

Mr. Adams: Are there any reactions to Colleen's comments?

Jerry: I think we've learned some of the same things. We've also discovered that we have to be a leader for quite a long period of time before we're really able to get the knack of it. Our group has tried to identify a certain task for which each of us provides leadership. That way we're all leaders at the same time but for different things.

Mr. Adams: So how is that working?

Jerry: We had some problems at first, especially coordinating things. But after we set up a schedule, we managed things better. Once you agree on a schedule, it's much easier to organize everything. We decided to do it this way because we anticipate that our learning project will take most of the year. That is the only way we could think of for sharing leadership responsibility.

Mr. Adams: It sounds like you are satisfied with your arrangement. Do other groups have anything to report?

Joan: In our group we have decided on three projects during the year. For each of these there are two leaders. Aaron came up with the idea. We thought it might be something educational to try. The basic idea is that with two leaders they can interact about their role frequently and perhaps give each other important feedback about what they are doing. You know the old adage that "two heads are better than one."

Jack: But out in the world there is usually just one leader. What about that?

Jerry: We've thought about that. It doesn't mean that's the way it should be. Besides, we are just learning about leadership. We all agreed that we could learn more about it with this format. We don't think what we are doing will keep us from learning what is necessary to be a solitary leader.

Mr. Adams: It appears that Jerry's group is not only involved in doing research in their learning projects; they are experimenting with learning community processes as well. Does anyone have any more feedback to give them?

Huia: I like their approach. I hope they will report on what they find out about it at the end of the year.

Mr. Adams: Actually, it may be appropriate for them to report on it much earlier. We should all benefit from the research of other groups as we go along. Are there any other comments?

Blair: I get concerned about that kind of leadership. How can you be sure you get everything done if no one individual is responsible?

Mr. Adams: Would you care to explain more of what you mean?

Blair: Well, in our group I have noticed that a lot of things don't get done when we try to have everyone act as leaders. We change leaders every two weeks. We thought that would give each person several chances to be a leader during the year and that each person could learn from other members of the group and then try out what is learned about leading the group. We've also set it up so we can give feedback to each other.

Mr. Adams: So, what do you do when you notice things are not getting done?

Blair: I just encourage others to do their part. If they don't get everyone to finish their part of the project on time, we won't be able to fit the different pieces together according to our schedule. Sometimes the group leader just doesn't make sure everyone does their part on time.

Mr. Adams: So when that happens you say you try to supply the necessary leadership?

Blair: That's right.

Mr. Adams: This sounds like an important concept to talk about. Does anyone have any input to give?

Huia: What I wonder about is what then happens to the person who is supposed to be the leader. What do they do?

Blair: I hope they would just take care of their responsibility.

Wayne: But what if they see their responsibility in a different way than you do?

Blair: Well, I don't know. It's just that things don't get done.

Peggy: I know how I feel when someone takes over for me. I just quit. Sometimes I even try to sabotage what they do and become very uncooperative. Is that what you notice with your group?

Blair: I never really considered that, but I guess you could be right. All I know is that we are getting further and further behind.

Mr. Adams: Think back about some of the things you learned at the first of the year. Which is most important, the learning process or the concepts we learn?

Carla: We all know the answer to that. We have to give them equal importance. That's because we learn as much from the process as we do from the content.

Klane: That's right. And I think with Blair's group they may need to look at that issue to see if it is being properly applied.

Blair: I thought I had been giving appropriate emphasis to process. I thought I was helping my group members see how a leader needs to make sure things get done.

Dwayne: But you just said that you are way behind in your project.

Blair: I get the point. And I guess you must be right. When I think about it, I think some of the group members do appear to resist my directions. It's just like Peggy says. I can see that now. The harder I pushed the more everyone resisted me.

Mr. Adams: It is true that there are multiple objectives in our learning community. It is hoped that you really master the learning process as well as the leadership role. It is also hoped that you learn how to have good relationships and learn to care about each other very much. Appropriate leadership can help both in learning as well as developing a sense of care. The suggestion that Blair's group spend some time examining their operations is a good one. The input given today may provide a few ideas for them. This and other related matters can be discussed in future classroom meetings. Please feel free to bring up any issue that you think needs attention. I think you are learning many things that could be beneficial to the entire class.

In the above example, Mr. Adams helps provide a focus as needed, but lets the class raise issues and discuss them without any more input from him than necessary. Even when he could teach a particular concept, he waits for students to bring the issue up and comment about it. His role is one of making sure that appropriate points are raised, that summaries of what has been discussed are included, and that any necessary clarifications are made. He also makes sure that there is class agreement regarding important factors.

In dealing with issues, Mr. Adams provides a model of leadership. Eventually he will need to furnish less input as students skillfully bring up and address important issues. A greater sense of community will arise as students learn to regulate their own behavior (Battistich, Solomon, Kim, Watson, & Schaps, 1995).

Democratic Discipline in Learning Communities

With democratic discipline, appropriate principles of an ideal democratic society are taught. Appropriate views of human nature are a critical part of this discipline approach. Most especially children's needs and learning inclinations should be thoughtfully addressed and should frame the nature of schooling. In a properly run learning community, the effects of excessive control and punishment are examined from the vantage point of available research, and applications made that properly employ appropriate principles.

It should be pointed out that in democratic societies, self-government doesn't necessarily prevail. There are many things that people are punished for and many decisions that are made by others, even when individuals could decide some of these issues for themselves. However, in a democratic classroom it is assumed that learning self-government can help students become more expert in living successfully in a democracy, that they don't necessarily have to become the victims of excessive control and punishment, and that such an approach greatly limits the number of instances of antisocial behavior.

In many institutions and in the job market there are numerous instances of excessive coercion and punitive correction strategies that are imposed on people who break laws or otherwise disrupt the flow of social well-being. It has become increasingly clear that such approaches limit productivity and spawn irrational reactions.

There are various views of the causes of social discord and crime, at least one being the imposition of excessive control and punishment. Much social improvement could possibly be realized if citizens were trained in the schools under conditions that emphasize social responsibility along with an attitude of care. The fact that this ordinarily isn't the case should be reason enough to carefully examine the schools' role in promoting aberrant social behavior.

Society generally could greatly benefit from such an examination. It has long been known that serving a prison sentence doesn't prepare inmates for a moral life in a democracy. In addition, punishments meted out by the courts do not really serve as effective deterrents to future unlawfulness. Similar consequences can be expected with punitive school discipline. Such a system fails to help prepare children for moral living in a democratic society.

References

Adams, M. (1990). *Beginning to read: Thinking and learning about print.* Cambridge, MA: MIT Press.

Aiken, W. M. (1942). *The story of the eight-year study.* New York: Harper.

Allen, L., Rogers, D., Hensley, F., Glanton, M., & Livingston, M. (1999). *A guide to renewing your school: Lessons from the league of professional schools.* San Francisco: Jossey-Bass.

Alvermann, D., Smith, L., & Readence, J. (1985). Effects of interactive discussion and the text type on learning counterintuitive science concepts. *Journal of Educational Research, 88,* 420–425.

Amabile, T. (1992). *A study of effects on creativity of commissioned and uncommissioned art work.* Unpublished manuscript, Brandeis University.

Ames, C., & Ames, R. (1981). Competitive versus individualistic goal structures: The salience of past performance information for casual attributions and affect. *Journal of Educational Psychology, 73,* 411–418.

Anderson, R. (1984). Role of the reader's schema in comprehension, learning, and memory. In R. Anderson, J. Osborn, & R. Tierney (Eds.), *Learning to read in American schools: Basal readers and content texts.* Hillsdale, NJ: Lawrence Erlbaum Associates.

Arlin, P. K. (1975). Cognitive development in adulthood: A fifth stage? *Developmental Psychology, 11* (5), 602–606.

Armstrong, T. (1998). *Awakening genius in classrooms.* Alexandria, VA: Association for Supervision and Curriculum Development.

Aronfreed, J. M. (1968). Aversive control and socialization. In W. J. Arnold (Ed.), *Nebraska symposium on motivation* (pp. 271–320). Lincoln: University of Nebraska.

Azrin, N., & Holtz, W. (1966). Punishment. In W. K. Honig (Ed.), *Operant behavior areas of research and application.* New York: Appleton-Century-Crofts.

Bandura, A. (1997). *Self-efficacy: The exercise of control.* New York: Freeman.

Banks, J. A. (2000). The social construction of differences and the quest for educational equality. In R. Brandt (Ed.), *Education in a new era* (pp. 21–45). Arlington, VA: Association for Supervision and Curriculum Development.

Battistich, V., Solomon, D., Kim, D., Watson, M., & Schaps, E. (1995). School as communities, poverty level of student populations, and students' attitudes, motives, and performance: A multilevel analysis. *American Education Research Journal, 32* (3), 627–658.

Beihler, R., & Snowman, J. (1990). *Psychology applied to teaching* (6th ed.). Boston, MA: Houghton Mifflin.

Benard, B. (1993). Fostering resiliency in kids. *Educational Leadership, 51* (3), 44–48.

Berne, E. (1966). *Principles of group treatment.* New York: Oxford University Press.

Beyer, L. A. (1998). Uncontrolled students eventually become unmanageable: The politics of classroom discipline. In R. E. Butchart & B. McEwan (Eds.), *Classroom discipline in American schools: Problems and possibilities for democratic education* (pp. 51–81). Albany: State University of New York Press.

Blau, P. M., & Scott, W. R. (1962). *Formal organization*. San Francisco: Chandler.

Blumenfeld, P., Puro, P., & Mergendoller, J. (1992). Translating motivation into thoughtfulness. In H. Marshall (Ed.), *Redefining student learning: Roots of educational change* (pp. 207–239). Norwood, NJ: Ablex.

Bogen, J. (1968). The other side of the brain: An appositional mind. In R. Ornstein (Ed.), *The nature of human consciousness*. San Francisco: W. W. Freeman and Company.

Bradley, M. J. (2003). *Yes your teen is crazy: Loving your kid without losing your mind*. Gig Harbor, WA: Harbor Press.

Brandt, R. (1992). On building learning communities: A conversation with Hank Levin. *Educational Leadership, 50* (1), 19–23.

Brendtro, L., Brokenleg, M., & Van Brockern, S. (1990). *Reclaiming youth at risk: Our hope for the future*. Bloomington, IN: National Educational Service.

Brophy, J. (1998). *Motivating students to learn*. Boston: McGraw-Hill.

Brophy, J. (2004). Perspectives of classroom management: Yesterday, today, and tomorrow. In H. Jerome Freiberg (Ed.), *Beyond behaviorism: Changing the classroom management paradigm* (pp. 43–56). Boston: Allyn & Bacon.

Brown, A. L., & Campione, J. C. (1994a). Guided discovery in a community of learners. In K. McGilly (Ed.), *Classroom lessons: Integrating cognitive theory and classroom practice*. Cambridge, MA: MIT Press.

Brown, A. L., & Campione, J. C. (1994b). Situated cognition and the culture of learning. In K. McGilly (Ed.), *Classroom lessons: Integrating cognitive theory and classroom practice*. Cambridge, MA: MIT Press.

Burden, P. R. (1995). *Classroom management and discipline*. White Plains, NY: Longman.

Butchart, R. E. (1998). Introduction. In R. E. Butchart, & B. McEwan (Eds.), *Classroom discipline in American schools: Problems and possibilities for democratic education* (pp. 3–14). Albany: State University of New York Press.

Butkowsky, I. S., & Willows, D. M. (1980). Cognitive motivational characteristics of children varying in reading ability: Evidence for learned helplessness in poor readers. *Journal of Educational Psychology, 72*, 408–422.

Cameron, J., & Pierce, W. D. (1994). Reinforcement, reward, and intrinsic motivation: A meta-analysis. *Review of Educational Research, 64*, 363–423.

Cameron, J., & Pierce, W. D. (1996). The debate about rewards and intrinsic motivation: Protests and accusations do not alter the results. *Review of Educational Research, 66*, 39–51.

Carreiro, P. (1998). *Tales of thinking: Multiple intelligences in the classroom*. York, ME: Stenhouse Publishers.

Chance, P. (1993). Sticking up for rewards. *Phi Delta Kappan, 74*, 787–790.

Chickering, A. W. (1969). *Education and identity*. San Francisco: Jossey-Bass.

Clifford, M. (1984). Thoughts on a theory of constructive failure. *Educational Psychologist, 19*, 108–120.

Clinchy, E. (2001). Needed: A new educational civil rights movement. *Phi Delta Kappan, 82* (7), 493–498.

Coleman, D. L. (2002). *Fixing Columbine: The challenge to American liberalism*. Durham, NC: Carolina Academic Press.

Condry, J. (1977). Self-initiated versus other initiated learning. *Journal of Personality and Social Psychology, 35*, 459–477.

Confrey, J. (1990). What constructivism implies for teaching. In R. Davis (Ed.), *Constructivist views on the teaching and learning of mathematics* (p. 109). Reston, VA: National Council of Teachers of Mathematics.

Coombe, K (1999). Ethics and the learning community. In J. Retallick, B. Cocklin, & K. Coombe (Eds.), *Learning communities in education: Issues, strategies and contexts*. New York: Routledge.

Coopersmith, S. (1967). *The antecedents of self-esteem*. San Francisco: W. H. Freeman.

Corso, J. (2005). Age and sex differences in thresholds. *Journal of Acoustical Society of America, 31*, 489–507.

Covington, M. V., & Beery, R. G. (1976). *Self-worth and school learning.* New York: Holt, Rinehart, & Winston.

Craske, M. (1985). Improving persistence through observational learning and attribution re-training. *British Journal of Educational Psychology, 55*, 138–147.

Crawford, B., Krajcik, J., & Marx, R. (1999). Elements of a community of learners in a middle school science classroom. *Science Education, 83* (6), 701–723.

Cronbach, L. J. (1963). *Educational psychology.* New York: Harcourt, Brace & World.

Csikszentmihalyi, M. (1990). *Flow: The psychology of optimal experience.* New York: Harper & Row.

Curwin, R., & Mendler, A. (1988). Packaged discipline programs: Let the buyer beware. *Educational Leadership, 46* (2), 68–71.

Darling-Hammond, L. (1997). *The right to learn: A blueprint for creating schools that work.* San Francisco: Jossey-Bass.

Dearden, R. F. (1975). Autonomy as an educational ideal. In S. C. Brown (Ed.), *Philosophers discuss education* (pp. 3–18). London: Mcmillan.

Deci, E. L. (1981). Effects of externally mediated rewards on intrinsic motivation. *Journal of Personality and Social Psychology, 18*, 105–115.

Deci, E., & Ryan, R. (1994). Promoting self-determined education. *Scandinavian Journal of Educational Research, 38*, 3–14.

Deci, E. L., Koestner, R., & Ryan, R. (1999). A meta-analytic review of experiments examining the effects of extrinsic rewards on intrinsic motivation. *Psychological Bulletin, 125* (6), 627–668.

DelBello, M. S. (1988, May–June). Fostering independent workers: A parent's view. *Gifted Child Today, 11*, 45–46.

Devine, T. (1987). *Teaching study skills: A guide for teachers* (2nd ed.). Boston: Allyn & Bacon.

DeVries, R., Hildebrandt, C., & Zan, B. (2000). Constructivist early education for moral devel-opment. *Early Education & Development, 11* (1), 9–24.

Duncan, G. & Brooks-Gunn, J. (1997). *Consequences of growing up poor.* New York: Russell Sage Foundation.

Dweck, C., & Elliot, E. (1983). Achievement motivation. In P. Mussen (Ed.), *Handbook of child psychology: Vol. 4. Socialization, personality, and social development* (4th ed.). New York: John Wiley & Sons.

Ebers, E., & Streefland, L. (2000). Collaborative learning and the construction of common knowledge. *European Journal of Psychology of Education, 15* (4), 479–490.

Eccles, J. S., Bachanan, C. M., Flanagan, C., Fuligni, A., Midgley, C., & Yee, D. (1991). Control versus autonomy during early adolescence. *Journal of Social Issues, 47* (4), 53–68.

Edwards, C. H. (1975). Variable delivery systems of peer-associated token reinforcement. *Illinois School Research, 12* (1), 19–28.

Edwards, C. H., & Allred, W. E. (1990). Autonomy in the classroom: The contrast between teachers' beliefs and students' perceptions. *Illinois School Research and Development, 26* (3), 186–196.

Edwards, C. H., & Surma, M. (1980). The relationship between type of teacher reinforcement and student inquiry behavior in science. *Journal of Research in Science Teaching, 17* (4), 337–341.

Elliot, C. (1971). Noise tolerance and extra-version in children. *British Journal of Psychology, 62* (3), 375–380.

Englander, M. E. (1986). *Strategies for classroom discipline.* New York: Praeger.

Engle, R. A., & Conant, F. R. (2002). Guiding principles for fostering productive disciplinary engagement: Explaining an emergent argument in a community of learners classroom. *Cognition and Instruction, 20* (4), 399–484.

Enzle, M. E., & Wright, E. F. (1992). *The origin-pawn distinction and intrinsic motivation.* Unpublished manuscript.

Epstein, J., & Harackiewicz, J. (1992). Winning is not enough: The effects of competition and achievement on intrinsic interest. *Personality and Social Psychology Bulletin, 18*, 128–138.

Erickson, M. F., & Pianta, R. C. (1989). New lunch box, old feelings: What kids bring to school. *Early Childhood Education and Development, 1*, 15–23.

Espelage, D. L., Mebane, S. E., & Swearer, S. M. (2004). Gender differences in bullying: Moving beyond mean level differences. In D. L. Espelage & S. M. Swearer (Eds.), *Bullying in American schools: A social-ecological perspective on prevention and intervention* (pp. 15–36). Mahwah, NJ: Lawrence Erlbaum Associates.

Fensham, P. (1992). Science and technology. In P. W. Jackson (Ed.), *Handbook of research on teaching* (p. 801). New York: Macmillan.

Fenstermacher, G. D. (1990). Some moral considerations on teaching as a profession. In J. I. Goodlad, R. Soder, & K. A. Sirotnik (Eds.), *The moral dimensions of teaching* (pp. 130–151). San Francisco: Jossey-Bass.

Fosnot, C. T. (1996). Constructivism: A psychological theory of learning. In C. T. Fosnot (Ed.), *Constructivism: Theory, perspectives, and practice*. New York: Teachers College Press.

Fox, D. S. (1994). Promoting resilience in students. *Thrust for Educational Leadership, 24*, 34–38.

Freedman, J. L., Cunningham, J. A., & Krismer, K. (1992). Inferred values and the reverse-incentive effects in induced compliance. *Journal of Personality and Social Psychology, 62*, 357–368.

Gardner, H. (1991). *The unschooled mind: How children think and how schools should teach*. New York: Basic Books.

Gardner, H. (1994). Multiple intelligences: A theory in practice. *Teachers College Record, 95* (4), 576–583.

Gardner, H. (2006). *Multiple intelligences: New horizons*. New York: Basic Books.

Gazzaniga, M. (1968). The split-brain of man. In R. Ornstein (Ed.), *The nature of human consciousness*. San Francisco: W. W. Freeman and Company.

Gibbs, B. (1979). Autonomy and authority in education. *Journal of Philosophy of Education, 13*, 119–132.

Ginott, H. (1971). *Teacher and child*. New York: Macmillan.

Glasser, W. (1984). *Control theory: A new explanation of how we control our lives*. New York: Harper & Row.

Glasser, W. (1986). *Control theory in the classroom*. New York: Harper & Row.

Glasser, W. (1990). *The quality school: Managing students without coercion*. New York: Harper and Row.

Glasser, W. (1997a). Choice theory and student success. *Education Digest, 63* (3), 16–27.

Glasser, W. (1997b). A new look at school failure and school success. *Phi Delta Kappan, 78* (8), 597–602.

Glasser, W. (1998). *Choice theory: A new psychology of personal freedom*. New York: Harper-Collins.

Glasser, W. (2005). *Every student can succeed*. Chatsworth, CA: William Glasser.

Glickman, C. D. (1993). *Renewing America's schools: A guide for school-based action*. San Francisco: Jossey-Bass.

Goldberg, M. D., & Cornell, D. G. (1998). The influence of intrinsic motivation and self-concept on academic achievement in second and third grade students. *Journal for the Education of the Gifted, 221(2)*, 179–205.

Good, T. L., & Brophy, J. E. (2000). *Looking in classrooms*. New York: Longman.

Goodlad, J. I. (1984). *A place called school: Prospects for the future*. New York: McGraw-Hill.

Goodlad, J. I. (2000). Education and democracy. *Phi Delta Kappan, 82* (1), 86–89.

Gose, B. (1997). Efforts to curb grade inflation get an F from many critics. *The Chronicle of Higher Education, 43*, A41–A42.

Greenberg, M. T., Kusche, C. A., & Speltz, M. (1991). Emotional regulation, self-control, and psychopathology: The role of relationships in early childhood. In D. Cicchetti & S. Toth (Eds.), *Rochester symposium on developmental pathology: Vol. 2. Internalizing and externalizing expressions of dysfunction* (pp. 21–55). Hillsdale, NJ: Erlbaum.

Greene, M. (1988). *The dialectic of freedom*. New York: Teachers College Press.

Harackiewicz, J. M., & Manderlink, G. (1984). A process analysis of the effects of performance-contingent rewards on intrinsic motivation. *Journal of Experimental Social Psychology, 20,* 531–551.

Harris, T. A. (1967). *I'm OK—you're OK.* New York: Avon Books.

Hartnett, D. N., Nelson, J. M., & Rinn, A. N. (2004). Gifted or ADHD? The possibilities of mis-diagnosis. *Roeper Review, 26* (2), 73–76.

Healy, J. (1990). *Endangered minds: Why our children can't think.* New York: Simon and Schuster.

Healy, J. (1994). *Your child's growing mind.* New York: Doubleday.

Hiatt, M., & Diana, B. (2001). School learning communities: A vision for organic school reform. *School Community Journal, 11* (2), 93–112.

Higgins-Trenk, A., & Gaite, A. (1971). Elusiveness of formal operational thought in adolescents. *Proceedings of the 79th Annual Convention of the American Psychological Association.*

Hobson, J. A. (1994). *Chemistry of conscious states.* Boston, MA: Little Brown and Co.

James, A. N. (2007). *Teaching the male brain: How boys think, feel, and learn in school.* Thousand Oaks, CA: Corwin Press.

Jelinek, J. J. (1979). A curriculum proposal for the development of maturity in students. (#ED 176286). Tempe: Arizona State University, Educational Research Information Center.

Jensen, L. C. (1985). *Adolescence: Theories, research, applications.* St. Paul, MN: West.

Kagan, J. M. (1994). *Galen's prophecy.* New York: Basic Books.

Kamii, C. (1984). Obedience is not enough. *Young Children, 39* (4), 11–14.

Kamii, C. (1991). Toward autonomy: The importance of critical thinking and choice making. *School Psychology Review, 20,* 382–388.

Keefe, J. W., & Jenkins, J. M. (2002). Personalized instruction. *Phi Delta Kappan, 83* (6), 440–448.

Keith, S., & Martin, M. E. (2005). Cyber-bullying: Creating a culture of respect in a cyber world. *Reclaiming Children and Youth, 13* (4), 224–228.

Koestner, R., Zuckerman, M., & Koestner, J. (1987). Praise, involvement, and intrinsic motivation. *Journal of Personality and Social Psychology, 53,* 383–390.

Kohlberg, L. (1969). The cognitive development approach to socialization. In D. A. Goslin (Ed.), *Handbook of socialization theory and practice* (p. 375). Chicago: Rand McNally.

Kohlberg, L. (1973). Continuities in childhood and adult moral development revisited. In P. Baltes & K. W. Shaie (Eds.), *Life-span developmental psychology: Personality and socialization.* New York: Academic Press.

Kohlberg, L. (1976). Moral stages and moralization: The cognitive-developmental approach. In T. Lickona (Ed.), *Moral development and behavior.* New York: Holt, Rinehart & Winston.

Kohn, A. (1992). *No contest: The case against competition.* Boston, MA: Houghton Mifflin.

Kohn, A. (1993a). Choices for children: Why and how to let students decide. *Phi Delta Kappan, 75* (1), 8–20.

Kohn, A. (1993b). *Punished by rewards: The trouble with gold stars, incentive plans, A's, praise, and other bribes.* Boston: Houghton Mifflin.

Kohn, A. (1996). *Beyond discipline: From compliance to community.* Alexandria, VA: Association for Supervision and Curriculum Development.

Kohn, A. (1998). *What to look for in a classroom.* San Francisco: Jossey-Bass Publishers.

Kohn, A. (1999). Constant frustration and occasional violence: The legacy of American high schools. *American School Board Journal, 186* (9), 20–24.

Kotulak, R. S. (1996). *Inside the brain.* Kansas City, MO: Andrews and McMeel.

Kounin, J. S., & Gump, P. V. (1961). The comparative influence of punitive and non-punitive teachers upon children's concepts of school misconduct. *Journal of Educational Psychology, 52,* 44–49.

Kowalski, R. M., Limber, S. P., & Agatston, P. W. (2008). *Cyber-bullying.* Malden, MA: Blackwell Publishing.

LeDoux, J. (1996). *The emotional brain.* New York: Simon and Schuster.

Lepper, M. R. (1983). Extrinsic reward and intrinsic motivation: Implications for the classroom. In J. M. Levine & M. C. Wang (Eds.), *Teacher and student perceptions: Implications for learning* (pp. 281–317). Hillsdale, NJ: Lawrence Erlbaum Associates.

Lepper, M. R., & Greene, D. (1975). Turning play into work: Effects of adult surveillance and extrinsic rewards on children's intrinsic motivation. *Journal of Personality and Social Psychology, 31*, 479–486.

Linder R. W. (1994). Self-regulated learning in correctional education students and its implications for instruction. *Journal of Correctional Education, 45* (3), 122–126.

Linder R. W., & Harris, B. (1993). Self-regulated learning: Its assessment and instructional implications. *Educational Research Quarterly, 16* (2), 29–37.

Lochel, E. (1983). Sex differences in achievement motivation. In J. Jaspars, F. D. Fincham, & M. Hewstone (Eds.), *Attribution theory and research: Conceptual development and social dimensions*. New York: Academic Press.

Madaus, G., Russell, M., Higgins, J. (2009). *Paradoxes of high stakes testing*. Charlotte, NC: Information Age Publishing.

Manaster, G. J. (1989). *Adolescent development: A psychological interpretation*. Itasca, IL: F. E. Peacock Publishers.

Matthews, M. R. (2000). Appraising constructivism in science and mathematics education. In D. C. Phillips (Ed.), *Ninety-ninth yearbook of the National Society for the Study of Education: Part I. Constructivism in education: Opinions and second opinions on controversial issues* (pp. 161–192). Chicago: The University of Chicago Press.

McNeil, L. M. (2000). Creating new inequalities: Contradictions of reform. *Phi Delta Kappan, 81* (10), 729–734.

Meier, D. (2002). *In schools we trust: Creating communities of learning in an era of testing and standardization*. Boston: Beacon Press.

Mercer, N. (2002). Developing dialogues. In G. Wells and G. Claxton (Eds.), *Learning for life in the 21st century: Socio-cultural perspectives on the future of education*. Oxford, UK: Blackwell.

Merrow, J. (2001). Undermining standards. *Phi Delta Kappan 83* (9), 653–659.

Milner, B. (1969). Psychological defects produced by temporal lobe excision. In K. Pribram (Ed.), *Brain and behavior*. London: Penguin Books.

Mogel, W. (2001). *The blessing of a skinned knee*. New York: Penguin.

Morgan, M. (1983). Decrements in intrinsic motivation among rewarded and observer subjects. *Child Development, 54*, 636–644.

Moriarty, B., Douglas, G., Punch, K., & Hattie, J. (1995). The importance of self-efficacy as a mediating variable between learning environments and achievement. *British Journal of Educational Psychology, 65*, 73–84.

Mullen-Rindler, N. (2003). *Relational aggression and bullying: It's more than just a girl thing*. Wellesley, MA: Center for Research on Women.

Nagel, M. C. (2005). Understanding the adolescent brain. In D. Pendergast & N. Bahr (Eds.), *Teaching middle years: Rethinking curriculum, pedagogy, and assessment* (pp. 650–676). Crows Nest, NSW, Australia: Allen & Unwin.

Newman, J. M. (1998). We can't get there from here: Critical issues in school reform. *Phi Delta Kappan, 80* (4), 288–294.

Nichols, S. L., & Berliner, D. C. (2007). *Collateral damage: How high stakes testing corrupts America's schools*. Cambridge, MA: Harvard Education Press.

Noddings, N. (1992). *The challenge to care in schools*. New York: Teachers College Press.

Noddings, N. (1993). *Educating for intelligent belief or unbelief*. New York: Teachers College Press.

Noddings, N. (2002). *Educating moral people: A caring alternative to character education*. New York: Teachers College Press.

Norton, D. L. (1970, November). The rites of passage from dependence to autonomy. *School Review, 79*, 19–41.

Ornstein, R. (1978). The split and the whole brain. *Human Nature, 1*, 83.

Osborne R. J., & Wittrock M. C. (1983). Learning science: A generative process. *Science Education, 67*, 489–508.

Pearson, P. D., & Iran-Negate, A. (Eds.) (1998). *Review of Research in Education: Vol. 23.* Washington, DC: American Educational Research Association.

Peck, S. (1987). *The different drum: Community-making and peace.* New York: Simon and Schuster.

Penfield, W. (1952). Memory mechanisms. *AMA Archives of Neurology and Psychiatry, 67,* 178–198.

Phelan, P., Davidson, A., & Cao, H. (1992). Speaking up: Students' perspectives on school. *Phi Delta Kappan, 73* (7), 695–704.

Phillips, D. C. (2000). An opinionated account of the constructivist landscape. In D. C. Phillips (Ed.), *Ninety-ninth yearbook of the National Society for the Study of Education: Part I. Constructivism in education: Opinions and second opinions on controversial issues.* Chicago: The University of Chicago Press.

Piaget, J. (1950). *Psychology of intelligence.* New York: Harcourt Brace.

Piaget, J. (1954). *The construction of reality in the child.* New York: Basic Books.

Piaget, J. (1970). *Science of education and psychology of the child.* New York: Orion Press.

Pianta, R. C. (1999). *Enhanced relationships between children and teachers.* Washington, DC: American Psychological Association.

Piatt, J. (1979). *Hemisphericity and divergent youth: A study of right brained students, their school problems and personality traits.* Unpublished doctoral dissertation, Brigham Young University, Provo, UT.

Pintrich, P. R., & Schunk, D. H. (1996). *Motivation education: Theory, research, and applications.* Englewood Cliffs, NJ: Prentice-Hall.

Pizzolato, J. E., & Slatton, Z. L. (2007). The function of family involvement in adolescents' aspiration achievement. In P. R. Zelick (Ed.), *Issues in the psychology of motivation* (pp. 81–95). New York: Nova Science Publishers, Inc.

Pomerantz, E., Altermatt, E., & Saxton, J. (2002). Making the grade but feeling distressed: Gender differences in academic performance and internal distress. *Journal of Educational Psychology, 94* (2), 396–404.

Qvortrup, J. (1997). Children, individualism, and community [Review of the book *The missing child in liberal theory: Towards a covenant theory of family, community, welfare and civic state* by John O'Neil]. *Childhood: A Global Journal of Child Research, 4* (3), 359–368.

Raywid, M. A. (1993). Community: An alternative school accomplishment. In G. A. Smith (Ed.), *Public schools that work: Creating community.* New York: Routledge.

Reeve, J. M. (2009). *Understanding motivation and emotion* (5th ed.). Hoboken, NJ: Wiley.

Reeve, J., & Deci, E. (1996). Elements of the competitive situation that affect intrinsic motivation. *Personality and Social Psychology Bulletin, 22,* 24–33.

Rennels, M. (1967). Cerebral symmetry; An urgent concern for education. *Phi Delta Kappan, 57,* 471–472.

Resnick, L., & Klopfer, L. (Eds). (1989). *Toward the thinking curriculum: Current cognitive research* [1989 yearbook of the Association for Supervision and Curriculum Development]. Alexandria, VA: Association for Supervision and Curriculum Development.

Rohrkemper, M., & Corno, L. (1988). Success and failure on classroom tasks: Adaptive learning and classroom teaching. *Elementary School Journal, 88,* 299–312.

Rooney, K. J., & Hallahan, D. P. (1988). The effects of self-monitoring on adult behavior and student independence. *Learning Disabilities Research, 3* (2), 88–93.

Rutter, M., Maughan, B., Mortimore, P., Quston, J., & Smith, A. (1979). *Fifteen thousand hours.* Cambridge, MA: Harvard University Press.

Ryan, R. M., & Deci, E. L. (2000a). Intrinsic and extrinsic motivations: Classic definitions and new directions. *Contemporary Education Psychology, 25,* 54–67.

Ryan, R. M., & Deci, E. L. (2000b). When rewards compete with nature: The undermining of intrinsic motivation and self-regulation. In C. Sansone & J. M. Harchkiewicz (Eds.), *Intrinsic and extrinsic motivation: The search for optimal motivation and performance* (pp. 13–54). San Diego: Academic Press.

Ryan, R. M., & Stiller, J. (1991). The social contexts of internalization: Parent and teacher influences on autonomy, motivation and learning. *Advances in Motivation and Achievement, 7,* 115–149.

Sansone, C., & Harackiewicz, J. M. (2000). Controversies and new directions—Is it Déjà Vu all over again? In C. Sansone & J. W. Horakiewicz (Eds.), *Intrinsic and extrinsic motivation: The search for optimal motivation and performance* (pp. 443–453). San Diego: Academic Press.

Sarason, S. (1990). *The predictable failure of educational reform.* San Francisco: Jossey-Bass.

Sax, L. (2005). *Why gender matters: What parents and teachers need to know about the emerging science of sex differences.* New York: Doubleday.

Scardamalia, M., & Bereiter, C. (1992). Text-based and knowledge-based questioning by children. *Cognition and Instruction, 9* (3), 177–199.

Schunk, D. (1985). Self-efficacy and classroom learning. *Psychology in the Schools, 22*, 208–223.

Seligman, M. E. P. (1995). *The optimistic child.* New York: HarperCollins.

Sergiovanni, T. J. (1990). *Value-added leadership: How to get extraordinary performance in schools.* San Diego, CA: Harcourt Brace Jovanovich.

Sergiovanni, T. J. (1992). *Moral leadership: Getting to the heart of school improvement.* San Francisco: Jossey-Bass.

Sergiovanni, T. J. (1994). *Building community in schools.* San Francisco: Jossey-Bass.

Sergiovanni, T. J. (1996). *Leadership for the schoolhouse.* San Francisco: Jossey-Bass.

Sergiovanni, T. J. (1999). The story of community. In J. Retallick, B. Cocklin, & K. Coombe (Eds.), *Learning communities in education: Issues, strategies and contexts* (pp. 9–25). New York: Routledge.

Sergiovanni, T. J. (2000). *The life world of leadership: Creating culture, community and personal meaning in our schools.* San Francisco: Jossey-Bass.

Simmons, A. (2002). *Odd girl out: The hidden culture of aggression in girls.* Orlando, FL: Harcourt.

Smith, D. (2004). *Bulletproof vests vs. the ethic of care.* Lanham, MD: The Scarecrow Press.

Smith, D., & Parrish, P. A. (2003). Prevention of school violence. In D. Smith (Ed.), *Bullet proof vests vs. the ethic of care* (pp. 77–92). Lanham, MD: The Scarecrow Press.

Smith, F. (1990). *To think.* New York: Teachers College Press.

Smith, F. (2001). Just a matter of time. *Phi Delta Kappan, 82* (8), 573–576.

Smith, J. O., & Price, R. A. (1996). Attribution theory and developmental students as passive learners. *Journal of Developmental Education, 19* (3), 2–4.

Smith, W. C. (1992). Hemispheric preference in the rise and fall of a business. In I. L. Sonnier (Ed.), *Hemisphericity as a key to understanding individual differences* (pp. 523–555). Springfield, IL: Charles C. Thomas Publishers.

Solomon, J. (1994). The rise and fall of constructivism. *Studies in Science Education, 23*, 1–19.

Sperry, R. W. (1974). Lateral specialization of cerebral function in the surgically separated hemispheres. In F. O. Schmitt & F. G. Worden (Eds.), *The neurosciences: Third study program.* Cambridge, MA: MIT Press.

Sperry, R. W. (1975). In search of psyche. In F. Worden, J. Swarzes, & G. Adelman (Eds.), *The neurosciences: Paths of discovery.* Cambridge, MA: MIT Press.

Starratt, R. J. (1996). *Transforming educational administration: Meaning, community, and excellence.* New York: McGraw-Hill.

Tauber, R. T. (1999). *Classroom management: Sound theory and effective practice* (3rd ed.). Westport, CT: Bergin & Carvey.

Trice, H. M., & Beryer, J. M. (1984). Studying organizational cultures through rites and ceremonials. *Academy of Management Review, 9* (4), 653–669.

Thal, D. J., Tobias, S., & Morrison, D. (1991). Language gesture in late talkers: A 1-year follow-up. *Journal of Speech and Hearing Research, 35* (6), 604–612.

Turner, J. C., & Meyer, D. K. (1995). Motivating students to learn: Lessons from fifth grade math class. *Middle School Journal, 27*, 18–25.

Walters, R., Parke, R., & Crane, V. (1965). Timing of punishment and the observation of consequences to others as determinants of response inhibition. *Journal of Experimental Child Psychology, 2*, 10–30.

Watkins, C. D. (2005). *Classrooms as learning communities: What's in it for schools?* New York: Routledge.

Weiner, B. (1992). *Human motivation: Metaphors, theories and research.* Newbury Park, CA: Sage.

Werner, B. (1990). History of motivational research in education. *Journal of Educational Psychology, 82*, 616–622.

Werner, E., & Smith, R. (1989). *Overcoming the odds: High-risk children from birth to adulthood.* New York: Cornell University Press.

White, R. (1959). Motivation reconsidered: The concept of competence. *Psychological Review, 66*, 297–333.

Wickett, R. E. Y. (2000). The learning covenant. *New Directions for Adult and Continuing Education, 35*, 39–47.

Wilkins, W. E. (1976). The concept of self-fulfilling prophesy. *Sociology of Education, 49*, 175–183.

Williams, J. E. (1996). The relation between efficacy for self-regarded learning and domain specific academic performance. *Journal of Research and Development in Education, 29* (2), 77–80.

Wilson, D. A., Willner, J., Kurtz, E. M., & Nadel, L. (1986). Early handling increases hippocampal long-term potentiation in young rats. *Behavioral Brain Research, 21*, 223–227.

Woollams, S., & Brown, M. (1979). *TA: The total handbook of transactional analysis.* Upper Saddle River, NJ: Prentice Hall.

Zito, J., et al. (2003). Psycotrophic practice patterns in youth. *Archives of Pediatrics and Adolescent Medicine, 157*, 17–23.

Index